The Still Small Voice Within

The Still Small Voice Within

Natalia Amuta Christos

Library of Congress Control Number: 2020901069
ISBN: Hardcover   978-1-7960-7230-3
                 Softcover   978-1-7960-7229-7
                 eBook   978-1-7960-7228-0

To order additional copies of this book, contact:
Xlibris
1-888-795-4274
www.Xlibris.com
Orders@Xlibris.com
805217

CONTENTS

A True Story

The names have been changed—and the places.

To the Lost as I Once Was, Jesus Is All About New Beginnings
This is dedicated to all the ones who have no hope, who have
been thrown to the side, unloved by the human race.

The rich man had everything he wanted, while the poor man sat at the gate, desiring the bread crumbs from the rich man—and literally got none.

What is the still small voice? It's the Spirit that Jesus said would come to help us, teach us, and protect us. Jesus said He could not be everywhere, but the Spirit—He can leave us be. The still small voice, when He does come, speaks what the Father has said to tell you. He cannot speak His own message to you. He has to stay inside the order of God, and the purpose is so you will know things to come for protection and guidance and to forewarn yourself and others. Wow! (John 16:13)

CHAPTER 1

Redeeming Us

It all started in the very foundations of the earth. He had and has a plan to redeem us from generational curses. He sent the angels to be the messengers. Even when we had no knowledge of knowing this, He was and is still there.

My desire is to be as Abraham, yet I totally love being a woman. With that said, I should say, "God, grant me the spirit of Abraham and all the faithful ones who lived before and after Jesus Christ. Your promise is to be grafted into every aspect of who you are, and your promises are for anyone who will just believe in the heart, confessing you are Lord of all and realizing we need you so deeply to penetrate through every fiber of our being. You are all we need. Yes, you! Thank you for the well-thought-out plan that you have provided. Abraham parted from his home and headed where you call him to go. And you blessed him beyond what he could think or imagine. He had land and lots of it. Animals of every kind filled his land that God so graciously gave to him."

Abraham is one of many amazing stories found in the Bible, and the contexts certainly are awe-inspiring to those who read it by the Spirit. They come alive, the promises and the goals that God placed in Abraham's heart and the hearts of all the saints. What a gift, to have a higher love for the Father God, to have no other gods before Him, and to be able to pass this down to generation after generation! Abraham's blessings fell on many nations all the way to us. The numbers go as far as the sand and stars, and it all started with his love for the Father from the Father. This is such good news, the promise of being grafted into the King of all Kings. The Messiah would come through his bloodline. This was foretold thousands of years before the foundations of the earth. Imagine that.

God has given us every opportunity to hear Him, whether it be in words or through the world in which we live. His creation is all around us. We are all given an account. Nothing was left undone. In my search, I find Him in the little things, and in those little things, I explode with gratitude. But we must choose to listen. He will answer you, I promise. His life continues to tell the world's greatest stories of humanity through Christ and the saints. (This means you too if you chose to be grated in.)

The promise of Abraham is the lineage to the King of all Kings, His glorious son, Jesus, and we can tap into this source through the Son. Wow—and to be able to live it out is so fantastic here on the earth! Life is not perfect here on the earth, yet we can rest in the truth and know that He is with us and He will not depart from us and, to top it all off, depart to go on and live forever with the Creator of all heaven and earth—heaven, where nothing grows old or rots.

Finally and suddenly, you see your very own storybook opened, and your heart and motives are exposed. The light of Jesus flows, and you hear the words come from the heavens: "Well done, my faithful servant!" You look around and see perfection, pure perfection, and all the saints and loved ones standing there with you in the celebration of your new beginning for all eternity, right there in the heaven. Jesus is found in the center of all things. Do you see Him? He gave us more than we could ever imagine. Our spirit is free to live in Him right now, no matter what you are facing. The joy of the Lord is my strength. For real, have you asked Him in your heart here now while you have life on Earth? I certainly hope so 'cause we are going to be just singing and praising the glory of the Lord forevermore. All aboard!

CHAPTER 2

The Little Red Sports Car

Getting intoxicated is my solution to the sadness. "Find your smile" were the words the two of us, me and a very dear friend in her last days of life, concluded with. It forced me to go deeper with the very lives we are given. She was looking for her smile. I realized life can be too serious. Relax and enjoy it. Lighten up. Smile even when you don't want to. Someone needs it. I like to look around and appreciate people, to pull my sunshine out of my pocket and share it now—right now. We sometimes take things for granted. A smile goes a long way. Smile more. Find your smile, even when you don't want to. We are alive now, so let's show it.

One day I went to visit a very dear friend whom I had the pleasure of meeting years ago at a workplace. She always had a smile and great advice. Reflecting back, I know the love that grew between us was very special. It was such an honor to know her and her lovely family. It was so great that she had whispered one day that I was like a daughter to her, and I was never to forget it. At that time in my own life, I was unwanted by someone near and dear to me. The feeling of being unwanted was the most incredible pain that I would not wish that even on an enemy.

So when my dear friend said, "You are like one of my daughters," my heart skipped a beat with joy.

I had lost my own mother at the age of twenty, and no one can take her place. We have only one mother. Yet her words filled my heart with gratitude and affection and with such appreciation of being needed. I truly miss her and my biological mother. ♥

She had a very special photo next to her bedside. She loved this photo. It filled her with such fond memories, and boy, did she share some good ones with me. This little red convertible belonged to her husband whom she adored. Yes, he owned one just like it many moons ago. She had gotten to where she was unable to leave her bed. One day I picked up the photo and asked her if she would like to go on an imaginary trip with me to the ocean in her little red car.

She thought this ought to be fun. "Why not? Let's go."

"Okay then. Grab your bag with a few things, and let's get out of here."

"All packed," she replied. "Lickety-split!"

"Wow, you're quick!"

We giggled.

"We are headed to the ocean. Wear a beautiful scarf to wrap your hair so the wind doesn't mess up your lovely long hair."

"Oh! Hmmm . . ." She rolled her eyes as if I were telling a story and said, "My hair is lovely?" She giggled.

"Absolutely. You are beautiful."

The bags were packed, and we hopped in for a lovely drive. We could talk about anything. We'd laugh. We'd cry. Neither one of us had any secrets.

"Oh, Ms. Daisy, the wind feels incredible on our faces, and the sun feels so amazing, doesn't it?"

She lifted her hands like a child and let the wind blow through her fingertips. The wind was strong and pushed her hand back and forth. She closed her eyes and said, "Yes. Yes, it does. It's a beautiful day to be with my friend."

"Yes, it is, Ms. Daisy. My sentiments as well."

"I bet the sand on our toes will be incredible too, Abigail."

"Boy, you bet! It sure will be great."

We both giggled.

By this time, we both had our eyes closed, dreaming of the escape to a more pleasant and powerful moment. Oh, the fun we had and the precious time spent together while she lay in her comfy bed!

One day the time was drawing near for her to be going to the Father (whom we talked about a lot). She did mention she had enjoyed the Bible stories I shared, and boy, did I share them! We cried, we laughed, and we imagined. I would play some Christian music and sing to her. She would close her eyes and quietly listen.

When I finished singing, these precious words flowed from her lips: "Something beautiful, just beautiful, is going to happen real soon. I feel it."

I started to sob. I thought she was letting go of this life and making her entrance to eternity. She had no more need for this life and was making her transition.

She opened her eyes and said, "Thank you for being my friend, my daughter, and by the way, has anyone told you lately that you are beautiful?"

I sat there, crying. "Oh, Ms. Daisy, your words are so sweet!"

Then she opened her eyes really wide and said, "Don't cut your hair. And you do need more curls."

I laughed and cried at the same time, if that is possible, and said, "Okay then. The next time you see me, I will have lots of curls just for you."

CHAPTER 3

Your Pearls . . . Be Careful Where You Cast Them; You Belong on the Shore

Oh, the stories found in life! I bet you have some great stories to tell as well. The scriptures are filled with life and amazing stories and totally help us understand what love really is, help us achieve the goals that we can believe in Christ in me, Christ in you, the hope of His glory that has been seen and will continue to be seen in humans. We are promised to be the very ones who are numbered by the stars and sand upon the shores. We are the stars and the tiny grains of sand. Christ tells us we are numbered and there are so many bursts of light and grains on the shore that it will be a difficult task to count. Can you count the stars and the sand? No, you can't. I can't. No human can. Only the Creator would be able to go there.

Changing the subject a tiny bit, do you know that a speck of sand in the oyster is really an irritant to the oyster, which forces the oyster to excrete a substance called nacre over and over, covering the sand, forming a beautiful pearl? It uses these minerals from the oyster's food to produce nacre, which goes on top of that tiny piece of sand or broken shell or a parasite that the oyster is irritated by. (That could symbolize all forms of humans, one an irritant, two a broken shell, three a parasite.)

All these situations can turn into opportunities. Do you choose to complain, or do you stop and let go? The oyster had to make the best of the irritation. We can't change people. Only God can do that. Let go. We all have irritating situations. Think of it as the making of your pearl. Jesus is the nacre that creates a smoothness inside us or, in this case, the oyster, which tolerates it, but it continues to grow because it notices it as a foreign object. Some people may be irritants to you, yet they really are creating a pearl for you. Our inheritance belongs to Christ, and we are as numbered as the sand.

We need to enjoy one another and learn how to help one another while we have time. Stop judging and love as Christ loves, and you certainly can have this promise too. Have what? The promise to be the burst of light to a lost or unhappy soul. Be one of the many grains of sand found on the shores, having it all through Christ, who gives us the strength to continue on. Share your smile. Oh, how He loves us!

CHAPTER 4

Inheritance Found in the Sand

Abraham was one of the early seeds who led us to Jesus. Abraham was one of the wealthiest in the inheritance of the human race (Christ being first, of course). He was found faithful in his understanding of the Messiah who was and is to come. He was granted the great power of discernment and enlightenment to act as he heard what God had told him to do. The faith was given to him through God, who wants us to be as one. The Holy Spirit helps us achieve that.

He became a leader through the obedience of love to the Father, who first loved us, and the knowledge and skill in dealing with hearing the voice of the Lord. Yet he was weak when Sarah gave him permission to sleep with Hagar. Oops . . . but see, it just goes to show that the human race will fail, but Jesus did not.

Wealth comes in many forms. The first of true wealth starts with the love and reverence for the King of Kings and the Lord of Lords. It all starts with wisdom that was with God in the beginning of the foundations of the earth! We must have fear (which, by the way, is worship), fear of the Creator and all that exist through Him, wisdom to know the difference to do the work of the Lord. His eyes are searching to and fro just as the enemy is searching to and fro. The Lord's eyes are searching for whom He can find faithful to bless to do His work before the return. Satan is also to and fro to whom he may destroy.

Abraham was granted by God to have offspring, as many as the numbers of the sand by the seas and the many stars in the sky. We all are tapping into this, whether you know the source or not, and we do have an inheritance to give and present to the King, just as Abraham was found faithful. Hallelujah! He fed the poor. He housed the poor. He told stories of the greatest love ever found to the poor. Who are the poor? A man can have everything and be poor. God has the power to give and to take away. He looks at the heart, the motive.

Christ has a need, and it is through us to reach the lost, the sick, the homeless, the ones who lost hope. Please join me to help in creating a sanctuary for such a dream, a vision—but obviously, first, with much prayer and for the purchase of land, a wonderful working farm far from the rat race of the world, a home with resources to help build the belief that those without hope are loved and have a purpose for life, a highly skilled web of people who will bring their talent to the table, to teach internet marketing skills, to help give the necessary skills to grow and provide a future to be self-sufficient, to love and train in the gift of working and being a good steward over time and money, paying with not only money but also self-worth, giving hope and appreciation of who we are in Christ, encouraging, edifying . . . and yes, sometimes we all need a soft rebuke.

The lost need help. God knows what we need of long before we ask for it. But my vision is massive, and where God leads, He provides. If He is in it, it will work, and I know He is in it. Why? Because He cares for the lost and wants them to know of His love for them. Life has many roads, and the heart of God is to be with you. Then who can stand against you or anyone who desires to have more?

The vision, the dream, the goal starts with a beautiful massive home (not a stale institute), with *a church* that has self-sufficiency with all manners of food—the whole nine yards. It must be housed with love, with a highly educated staff who love the Lord and His fullness thereof, with amazing, loving people who know how to help and treat the lost and help them be found, to build in them a hope, a sense, and a sure foundation of knowing who they are and how they have a gift that was given to each and every one at their birth that they know they have something to offer, that they have self-worth. *Do you see it? Do you see it?*

Let's sweep the countryside and offer the love the Father sees in them. Are you in? Of course, you are! We cannot take any material thing with us when we leave, but we do take what we have done to love others and help humans find value in who God says they are. So many are kicked down and need answers. Jesus wants to break the chains that have them bound.

Remember, our plans are small compared to the God above, who knows all things, who owns it all, from you and me to the flowers and the trees, the fish in the sea, the birds and the bees, and everything in between. Good news: we can do all things in Christ Jesus who strengthens us. Nothing is impossible to our God. So let us yolk up, and we can imagine the possibility of the greatness of His plan. Let's do this!

America needs hope. We are failing the younger generation. The soldiers have fought for our country only to come home and live in the streets. This is awful! Pray big time, for prayer changes things. God's face will shine upon you. He will bless us and keep us.

Some food for thought (❤):

- One gives freely yet grows all the richer; another withholds what he should give and only suffers want. (Proverbs 11:24 ESV)
- Let no one seek his own good but the good of his neighbor. (1 Corinthians 10:24 ESV)

Father, thank you for loving me. Thank you for sharing. Thank you for caring.

CHAPTER 5

Why Are You Here?

Elijah seeks the face of the Lord, and a great wind crumbles the mountain. Then an earthquake creates a fire as the Lord passes Elijah. The mountains crumble, the earthquake produces fire, and then, suddenly, a small voice is heard—"Why are you here?"

You are reading this book because the Lord brought you here. The still small voice, the Spirit of truth—the world will not know Him or accept Him, but you, you know Him because He lives in you. "I love you whether you choose to love me. Those who choose to know me, I will know you, and I will show myself to you. I will come and make a home with you." These words belong to my Father. We are given an advocate for the Father's gift—Jesus, who stands in our place—and the Holy Spirit, who will teach us more than we could ever know on our own. He remains with us through the words I (God) have spoken.

He forewarns us, "The prince of the earth is coming who has no hold on me (Jesus)!" The reason the prince (Satan) of this world comes is to show the world that what I have said is true. These are the Lord's words.

CHAPTER 6

First Lesson: You Have to Get the Root; This Is Deliverance

It was late winter, and the snow had melted away. The earth that was once frozen was giving us the first signs of life. The daffodils were in full bloom. Not trailing far behind though were the weeds. They were trying to drown out the beauty of the flowers that were offered for our enjoyment.

Mom was always ahead of her game. She didn't waste any time. She was on her knees, pulling up the unwanted weeds she called thieves. I decided I would help. I got right beside her and began to pull. I didn't say a word. I knew she was very busy. I started to think, *I am working well, and look! I have gotten so much done!*

About that time, she looked over at me. "Oh my! Do you realize you are making the plant stronger?"

"How? I have pulled up all these leaves, Momma. Look at all of them."

I was beaming, and I didn't understand what she was saying. However, my prideful thoughts stopped in their tracks when she said, "Honey, thank you for helping, but you are not helping."

"What? What do you mean?"

"You sure do have a huge pile of leaves. But do you have any roots? Roots are what make the plant strong. By pulling the leaves, you have made the plant stronger. Weeds will take over before you know it. They grow faster than the plants you want. You have to stay on top of it, or all you will have is a bed of weeds. And they will choke out the life of the good plant. The roots of the weed will store all the energy, and the weed will come back even stronger."

"Oh . . ." I was feeling kinda sad at that moment.

Momma took the hand tool and pushed it down deep and loosened the soil, and she exposed the roots. "You have got to get the root to kill the weed."

I was totally amazed, and now it made perfect sense. I have taken this same concept into my adult life. Life is a flowerbed. You may have weeds growing, and they are trying to choke out the very thing you wish to bring to life: a dream, a new business, a friendship, a book. Troubles (thoughts that don't line up with the Word of God) are the weeds that try to choke the life from the dream. Scripture is so clear that we can grow. We just have to get to the root that is the cause of the problem and root it out.

What a precious gift my mother gave me many years ago as we were on our knees, pulling weeds! I love you, Momma. You left me far too soon.

CHAPTER 7

The Gift of a Son

A true gift for any father! I had the honor of hearing a story that melted my heart, and it flowed from the lips of a very proud father. I literally walked away in tears knowing how much he loved his only son and how proud he was of *all* his children.

I mentioned, "Life is the gift. The ultimate gift, as you know. You are precious and bought with a price. All life is given by the grace of God. We are born so that we may truly live. Do you know Jesus?"

He told me a story about a dog he and his family loved. "We buried him under the magnolia. The tree was there for years and never bloomed. The loss of our pet broke our hearts. We truly missed him. He was laid to rest under our magnolia. And He, Jesus, brought us unexpected gifts year after year. Magnificent, massive, fragrant magnolia blooms. It was like I completely understood the seriousness of God's love for us. The flowers were tucked in the everlasting evergreen of hope with the tear-shaped leaves. Death can do that, make one think. The blooms were beautiful and had such a wonderful fragrance. The tree drew me in to have conversations with God. I know God was speaking to me through the burial of our pet, symbolizing the beauty of the tree, and I quietly listened to what He was saying from my kitchen picture window."

"What did God say?"

"Well, I can't tell you all of it, but that was my circle, my place of conversation."

"Wow! That is really special. The Father does have a way to communicate to us."

"It is very good, personal, and special."

"Oh, okay. I understand. Thank you for sharing that. It's a great story. God is pretty amazing, absolutely perfect to bring the blooms to remind you of your beloved pet and so much more. Wow!"

"Yes, God is out there tugging on my heart."

"You mean like a still small voice."

"Sure, it was. Jesus's stories keep giving, even after the death of a dear dog! His name is carried on through all things, especially those that we love, and His lesson to me showed me to believe in the beyond. I've been pretty quiet about my faith. It's not something I talk to many people about. It was something we were taught to believe but really didn't share. But . . . He loves us either way."

"So you carry on in the name of the Son, just as your son will continue to carry your name. Your son gave your name a future. And God's Son does just that too and so much more, the past, present, and future of all the good and perfect gifts that rain on us from heaven. Yay!" ♥

"I know that my heart felt the importance of wanting to give the gift of a son so that the husband's name can carry on too. As so many others feel this strong need."

"And God granted you your wish, Mr. Daisy. Your dream came true. He is so very good, Mr. Daisy."

He turned and wiped the tears from his eyes. He knew that he was blessed beyond happiness, yet he was very sick. "Now all I wish for is to hang on to see the birth of a precious granddaughter."

He did, but I do remember asking Mr. Daisy if he wouldn't mind doing me a big favor.

"Well, it depends. What's that?"

"If you happen to make it to heaven before I do"—he didn't think he had much time left—"please . . . My father left three years ago to be with the Lord. Will you introduce yourself to my dad? And give him a huge hug and also . . . This is a big request . . . Please give him a kiss and say hello to him like you were me and thrilled to see him. Please? For me, right there in heaven, and tell him I miss him. In fact, I expect my father to greet you and say hello to you. I believe he will know you without a word, and you will know him as well. What a glorious day! Both of you in your youth once more forevermore—that's what I am talking about!"

"Sure thing," he replied and then said, "Do you really think it will be just as you said, him knowing me without an introduction?"

"Yes. Yes, I do."

He puffed on that cigarette, smiled, wiped his tears, and said, "I know one thing for sure. The birth of each child gave my wife and I great joy. We did wonder if we would have the son to carry my name. And then the long-awaited day finally came. Abigail, I was overflowing and wanted to share these feelings of excitement and to tell the world that I was finally a father to a son. My heart was full. My name would live and would not die."

"Yeah, I am sure men can relate to this, Mr. Daisy. It was perfect, absolutely a perfect gift that your heart's desire was filled from the Father."

He beamed as his words poured out of his heart. Precious . . . he really wanted to do something really unique. "Long ago on that day, it was like a powerful hurricane. The hand of God had blanketed the earth with freshly fallen snow from the storehouses of heaven. I remember it as if it were yesterday. It was a winter wonderland. My playground to show the world and to thank the love of my life, Rose, and God. My gift from God, hand-knitted by the Creator in her safe place, the womb. The gift of a son."

The thankfulness poured from his heart, and he had to do something unique and wonderful. He was thinking to himself, *I love to fly. It gives me such peace to soar. There is nothing like it. You should try it sometime. Have you ever flown? You should have someone take you up about 1,000 to 1,500 feet and look down at the earth. There is nothing like it. Being in the seeming endlessness of the atmosphere. I am free . . . free as a bird."*

Meanwhile, I wondered why. Why did God bless me to hear these words from his lips about that glorious day that the father felt and relate it to so many wonderful things?

- The death of a dog
- The everlasting evergreen
- The magnolia blooms
- The personal conversations with the Creator
- The birth of Christ
- The safe place of a womb
- The carrying of his name

To feel his excitement to be granted a son—his heart was so full as he reminisced. This son was the last child to be born into this amazing, highly talented family.

You can imagine a woman wanting to give birth to a son to carry on the husband's name. The day came, with her not knowing what she was carrying. No ultrasound or 3-D here. It was a wait-and-see thing. She went into a long labor, and finally, news reached the dad.

"Surprise! You are a father to a beautiful baby boy."

Oh, how he rejoiced! It was a December day, and the newly fallen snow blanketed the earth. So overjoyed, he took his feelings to the open air with the wings of his aircraft. Soaring high, he dropped dozens of fresh long-stemmed roses to the earth near the grounds of the hospital, where his children lay snuggled in the arms of his true love. Oh, the gift of life—how precious it is!

Then Ms. Daisy shared her version. "You know back in the days of the birth of a baby, the husbands and family were not allowed in the delivery room?"

"Yes, of course."

"Having a baby was a big thing, and you had to stay in the hospital for weeks."

"Yes, my mother told me that too."

"The hospital I was in was a large building. I say that because I remember the nursing staff came running into the room, carrying some long-stemmed red roses. Oh, the excitement! 'Ms. Daisy! Ms. Daisy! Oh my gosh, come look out the window!' The ground had a fresh coat of pure white snow. And then . . . I could not believe my eyes. There were beautiful red roses everywhere, as far as the eye could see. Hundreds of them! And the nurses were outside, gathering some of them. Among the long stems were strudels of just the red petals as well. It was such a heartfelt moment. I could see in my daughter's eyes that they were thrilled to see the beauty of the love their father expressed to us, his family, that day. It was really special, to say the least. And quite the talk of the town, I might say."

"Wow, Ms. Daisy! That is so beautiful. It reminds me of the love of the Father, who lives in heaven. The snow that blew in that day to cover the ground made it white. That is what Jesus promised to us. He makes us white as snow when we ask forgiveness for our sins. The Son was born to cover us. Our name goes on. The red roses covered in thorns remind us of the crown that was given to the King. The petals are the blood that was shed for our multiple sins. Wow! God, why are you sharing this with me? Thank you. Mr. and Mrs. Daisy, when I write my book, I need to include this story. May I?"

"Sure." With a soft smile, they replied, "You may."

CHAPTER 8

Blessings Come When Putting Others First

For it will be like a man going on a journey, who called his servants and entrusted to them his property. To one, he gave five talents, to another two, to another one, to each according to his ability. Then he went away. He who had received the five talents went at once and traded with them, and he made five more talents. So also, he who had the two talents made two talents more. But he who had received the one talent went and dug in the ground and hid his master's money. (Matthew 25:14–30 ESV)

Fear gripped the one with one talent, afraid he would lose the one and buried it—absolutely *no* faith. I've done this, and when I do, I am sick with guilt that I missed the opportunity. Now in my grievance, I repent and ask forgiveness and to make me strong and see with your eyes, Father. What was I thinking? I wasn't.

An example of this is I needed a car for Norman, my fourth son, to get back and forth to college. My second son, Preston, totaled out another one of his cars. Oops! I went to pay the tow fee.

I was asked, "Why would you do that?"

"Do what?"

"Pay the bill."

"Well, let me ask you a question. If you went to the trouble of getting someone's wrecked car, I believe you would want to be paid for the work. Right? That is why I am going to pay the man's wages that are due him. Deuteronomy 24:15 says we are to pay his wages each day because he could be poor, and he counts on it, lest he cry against you—and trust me, that would be bad. For God will hear the cry. You must not withhold until morning the wages due a hired hand. Unless you have made a different agreement. And in this case, there isn't. He has done the work and needs his money. If I do what is right, I am allowing God to take care of the rest."

As I stood there at the counter to pay the fee, I asked, "Do you happen to have a car that no one picked up and didn't pay their bill? A left-behind car? I need a car for my son."

"Well . . . actually, my boss is trying to sell one of his. He is about to be back from lunch in a moment. He is in the car he wants to sell."

I waited. Within five minutes, he was back at the shop, and there he was in the car that was for sale. I stared in horror. It was a Cube. Can you say, "Oh no"? I couldn't do that to my son, even though the mileage was great and it took $20 to fill it up. Wow! It did sound like a great deal. It was so clean and in such perfect shape. But it tore at my heart that it would be awful for Levi. Can you imagine bringing a car like that home for your son to drive? Just saying. It felt like . . . *sooo* not the right opportunity.

But I flat out told Mr. Tron, "I could not do that to my son!"

He understood and said, "Oh, hold on. I have a car that I bought my wife, and she didn't drive it much. In fact, it stays at the shop for emergencies only. Let me get one of my guys to roll it around."

And there it was, a Mercedes 1999 with twenty-six thousand miles on it, in mint condition.

He said, "Hop in, and let's take it for a drive."

I said, "Okay. What can it hurt?"

It drove like a dream, so smooth. We got back to the shop, and he mentioned how much he needed for the car. It sounded so amazing.

I looked at him and said, "I love the car. It's beautiful. But the maintenance on it will be too high. This is a rich man's car. Thank you, but I am going to pass."

He continued to say, "You need this car. It is very reliable. I want you to get this car."

I was thankful, but I still wasn't going to do it.

He said, "If maintenance is the problem, you bring this car back into my shop, and we will fix it for you for as long as you own it!"

Now if one can ask this question nicely, I did. "What if you die? Then what?"

He said, "My men have been with me for many years. I will keep the shop open for them. They have families to take care of. Even when I am gone, I will continue to take care of them. And you can bring the car in, and they will take care of you."

The name Tron means balance. *Wow!* I thought, *This is love, love for his people who have been such a blessing to him that he wants to take care of them even when he is gone. Wow! So precious . . . . Now that is a good man.* I was amazed at his persistence. It seemed as though he was not going to take no for an answer. I told him I would certainly think about it, and I left.

He called me several times, wanting me to have the car. He even called his bank to have the manager call me. "Hmmm . . ." I continued to say, "It sounds wonderful, but . . ."

Some time passed. I felt led to send a letter of thanks for all the trouble he went through, talking with his bank and all. I was writing the letter, sitting at my mother-in-law's house, and the phone rang.

This time, he said, "I know a man who comes into my shop to buy cars occasionally. He heard the Mercedes-Benz was finally for sale. And he came to the shop to buy it. This is your last chance to have this car."

I said to him, "You sure want me to have this car, don't you?"

He said, "Yes, yes, I do. You seem like a lady who needs a good car."

Wow! I was touched.

He also said, "The man is coming this week to get it if I don't sell it to you. Bottom line, he will be making a profit, and he doesn't care for the car. It's all about profit. I know you need a car. And I know you will appreciate it. And it will be a great car for you. I paid a lot for it, and for some reason, I want someone who needs it and will appreciate it. And I believe you are the one."

I literally wanted to cry in gratitude.

Then he said, "Look, I will even come down $2,000."

I was visiting with my mother-in-law (who, by the way was shy sixteen days of a hundred years old!), who heard the whole conversation. I told her everything after I got off the phone.

She looked at me and said with all seriousness, "It sounds to me like God wants you to have this car. Go and buy it, Abigail. Tell him right now that you want it."

I thought about it and realized she was right, so I bought it! I was so thankful. When I had a need for a car, God provided—and I had never expected such a beautiful one. Then it seemed everywhere I went, cars were falling from the sky—not really, but great deals were everywhere, and I turned them down. As I thought about it, I could have bought them and resold them, making a lot of money!

I had even asked God jokingly, "Am I in the car business?"

Yes, I was, but I missed it. Hmmm. I am human. This is why I desperately need Jesus.

Note: The one thing I had noticed was that a confession was made out of my mouth on what the Lord had to say about certain situations if that lined it up with the Word of God and married my heart to my mind and became one in my thinking. Good or bad, it would manifest. This is why the Lord said to guard your mouth, for out of it are your issues in life. It is a belief that you know as truth—or not. You have to be careful. Does that make sense?

I know and believe this is why when I became a born-again believer, this was one of the first things the Lord showed me. It is the spiritual law that Christ has set in motion. The very first thing after I had asked Jesus into my heart, He asked me through the scriptures to renew my mind, just as He does with all new believers. It is important to get in the scriptures and see what the Lord is saying to you. We have to get rid of the old thinking. We are new. We don't pour old milk with new milk into a container. Otherwise, you could spoil the whole bottle of milk. We want fresh milk. That is actually what it is like, renewing the mind.

But how was I going to do that? You just let go and let Him talk with you through the Word. Through His word? Yes, trust Him, and He will help you. Action is required on your part. He was cleaning my house (meaning body) and my thinking and literally removing anything that was not from Him—songs, books, words, and so on. I was delivered from smoking, cussing (I didn't say too many bad words; I had one that was my favorite)—gone, just like that. I will tell you later in the book how that came about. Wow! God is real!

CHAPTER 9

The Still Small Voice from Within

God speaks. "Today, if you hear my voice, do not harden your hearts and deny me Jesus's words!" Jeremiah hears the still small voice: "Demolish and then start over." Jeremiah hears the voice of the Lord. He is given a job in advance. He is on a mission.

In Jeremiah 1:1–46:13, God tells Jeremiah, "I have set you over nations. I need you to uproot and destroy the kingdoms. They have to be rebuilt, and you are the one I have chosen to do just that." Can you imagine the Lord saying this to you?

Jeremiah knew the word and was of strong character. God had been talking to him for some time. It wasn't a one-time conversation; it was months that carried over to several reigns. In fact, God began to tell him that he knew him even before He had shaped him in his mother's womb.

"You had not even seen the light of day. But . . . I knew you, and I had plans to make you a prophet to the nations. Yet you told me, God, that you are just a boy. You think you are not able. But I tell you, you are! And I will go before you, and I will give you the words to say."

He continues to tell the Lord that he is just a boy.

God assures him that He will be with him. "They will try to fight you, but I will make you as strong as a steel beam. I will be there, and I will help you." God even goes as far to touch his mouth and hand-deliver the words. "I've just hand-delivered my words." God asks him, "What do you see?"

"I see a stick."

"Good eyes!" God said. "I am sticking with you no matter what, and we got the victory. Stand at attention. You are a one-man system. They'll fight you, but they won't even scratch you. And I am going to back you up every inch of the way."

God decrees this and more. Wow! We can have these kinds of conversations with the Lord. I have, and I love to hear from Him, and you can too. He had this same conversation with Moses, and Moses told God that he can't speak,

But God tells Moses, "You can because I will give you the words." Moses continues to argue with the Lord, and the Lord tells him, "I made you. I think you can." Still, he refuses. Finally, the Lord tells him to take Aaron, his brother, to do the talking for him then, and he did. But can you imagine having a debate with the Lord and telling Him you can't? We should rest in the following words and trust. What shall we then say to these things? If God be for us, who can be against Him? God knows you. We all are given the still small voice. It is His gift.

These words are found in the scriptures. Please look it up for yourselves. Always take everything with a grain of salt and weigh it out with the Word of God.

> When the Spirit of truth comes, He will guide you into all the truth. Just as He has done for me. The Spirit will not speak on his own authority but what God has ordained to be released to tell you. The great news is that He will declare to you the things that are to come. Just as He has done for me and others! Hallelujah! Hallelujah! Hallelujah! (John 16:13)

CHAPTER 10

Time for Mass

It was Sunday morning, and the River bunch (all nine of us) were headed to mass, a traditional service that I knew like clockwork. It seemed to me that we all filed in the mass and did exactly everything as we were told to do. We followed the order that we had been taught from the very beginning of our childhood. The nuns and the priest played a big part in the church, obviously. It was quite a show. The altar boys entered slowly down the long path leading to the altar with a reverence of awe to the God of heaven and earth. The long white gowns, trimmed in red, flowed toward the floor. Each boy carried a giant golden pole with a single burning candle from each. Everyone's eyes were on them.

We all knew what to do next. I suppose things have to stay within the long traditional way of doing things, reciting prayers at certain times, kneeling at a certain time, praying, and listening. Nothing happened out of the norm. Every Sunday's mass was the same, like clockwork.

I found myself wandering off as I stared at the stained-glass windows. They seemed to come alive with the beautiful story of the life of Christ. As I looked around the building, I wondered, *How many people here really know you? How many take to heart your message? How many really have a true knowing and worship of who you are?* I personally did not.

I was thinking, *I am certainly far away from God. But I want to be close. But after all, heaven is not really seen. I am just sitting here, imagining you on your throne, soaring in the wide-open, never-ending wholeness of the universe, your mysterious place where some by choice and others forced by parents come to hear stories of you from the past, present, and future. I am hopeful that you are looking down and do love me even with all my flaws.*

The pews and church seem cold to me. But I do have a heart to want to know you more with all knowledge of the mysteries that you hold while millions of questions dance around in

my head. Are you an intangible God? Do you have a big stick for those who are stiff necked? Are
you tender? How can I behave properly at all times? Is it even possible? Is there hope?

Hmmm . . . Wow! Children's minds do wander. I mentioned before what I
had noticed about God talking with Jeremiah when he was thirteen.

"What do you see?"

He responded, "A walking stick, that's all."

God told him, "Good eye! I am sticking with you. I will make you able. And
you will know what to say when to say it because I will work through you."

Wow! God has now removed the fear from Jeremiah, and he can be confident
that God is going to *stick* beside him, just do as asked. God is so good and foretells
the future to Jeremiah, and it *all* comes to pass. How cool is this? Amazing, I tell
you—amazing! That is God's message basically to the boy.

> Then the Word of the Lord came unto me, saying, "Before
> I formed thee in the belly, I knew thee, and before thou camest
> forth out of the womb, I sanctified thee, and I ordained thee a
> prophet unto the nations." Then said I, "Ah, Lord God! Behold,
> I cannot speak, for I am a child." But the Lord said unto me,
> "Say not, 'I am a child,' for thou shalt go to all that I shall send
> thee, and whatsoever I command thee, thou shalt speak. Be
> not afraid of their faces, for I am with thee to deliver thee,"
> saith the Lord. Then the Lord put forth His hand and touched
> my mouth. And the Lord said unto me, "Behold, I have put
> my words in thy mouth. See, I have this day set thee over the
> nations and over the kingdoms, to root out and to pull down and
> to destroy and to throw down, to build, and to plant. Moreover,
> the Word of the Lord came unto me, saying, "Jeremiah, what
> seest thou?" And I said, "I see a rod of an almond tree." Then
> said the Lord unto me, "Thou hast well seen, for I will hasten
> my word to perform it." And the word of the Lord came unto
> me the second time, saying, "What seest thou?" And I said, "I
> see a seething pot, and the face thereof is toward the north."
> Then the Lord said unto me, "Out of the north, an evil shall
> break forth upon all the inhabitants of the land. For lo, I will
> call all the families of the kingdoms of the north," saith the
> Lord, "and they shall come, and they shall set everyone his
> throne at the entering of the gates of Jerusalem and against all
> the walls thereof round about and against all the cities of Judah.
> And I will utter my judgments against them, touching all their
> wickedness, who have forsaken me and have burned incense
> unto other gods and worshipped the works of their own hands.

Thou, therefore, gird up thy loins and arise and speak unto them all that I command thee. Be not dismayed at their faces, lest I confound thee before them. For behold, I have made thee this day a defenced city, an iron pillar, and brasen walls against the whole land, against the kings of Judah, against the princes thereof, against the priests thereof, and against the people of the land. And they shall fight against thee, but they shall not prevail against thee, for I am with thee," saith the Lord, "to deliver thee." (Jeremiah 1:4–19 KJV)

I find it interesting that we are commanded to have no fear of the evil that is before us. And guess what? We all have fear at some point and time. But as the Lord said, they (all things that might have its grip on you) shall not prevail, for He is with us and will deliver us. This is good news.

CHAPTER 11

The Nuns . . . God Loves Them!

The nuns wore jet-black laced boots that stuck out from under their long creamy gowns that fell to their ankles and serious head coverings that literally were so tight so as not to expose one piece of hair on their heads. It circled the face, only exposing the foreheads, cheeks, nose, and mouth. (I again wondered, *What the heck? Do they even have hair? And if so, what color? How long is it?* Oh my! How can a young girl learn, thinking all these thoughts?)

They wore simple ropes, like belts, with giant light brown wooden crosses that just dangled at their side, and each sister had a silver ring on the marriage finger. Sitting at the desk I was assigned, I wondered about all kinds of strange things about them. The outfit was a hard one to get past—and the silver ring! *Are they really all married to Jesus? How can that be? Hmmm.*

Each classroom had a long wooden ruler that sat on the corner of the nun's desk. During question-and-answer time, you had better have the correct answers when asked. The nun or sister (as we would call her) would walk the aisles, tapping the ruler in her hand, and if she found one who was an offender, she would smack it hard on the desk of the guilty one. It was frightening for sure, and this was my early concept of what God might possibly be like—very strict, to say the least, enforcing the rules, all requirements, and your obligations to be in order at all times in and out of His presence, a judge who rigorously enforces and maintains at all times—and you'd better be still and silent or else.

Is that even possible to attain? Especially for a child? Hmmm . . . If any giggle erupted or if a slightly happy face came out, one would know better for sure—out with happy expressions. It was not allowed. Put on your serious face. Do you hear laughter in this room? No, not none. Run—run for your lives! Getting out seemed the only answer. Being at the tender age of six or seven, I recall begging my mother not to send me back, and she didn't. Looking back, I probably should have stayed. I would have been smarter, at least.

> A merry heart doeth good like medicine, but a broken spirit drieth the bones. (Proverbs 17:22 KJV)

Even as a child, I knew that this whole concept of their teaching was not for me at least. I was more on the creative side. I figured this could not be good for anyone. But what did I know? *Nothing.* It was oppressive and controlling but probably made a great learning environment. The Catholics were good at producing intelligent, superior students. Really! Thank you for that. I just couldn't do it.

It does appear that this wasn't a good fit for me. Everything around me said, "It can't be done." Have you ever heard that if zero goes in, zero is the return? When a child is bored and does not make the connections as to why this is important, it then becomes nothing in return (zero). I certainly felt like a butterfly trapped in my cocoon, wanting out. It was an oppressive and controlling spirit that was present. Learning in that kind of sitting well frightened me.

One must learn with a joyful heart, and if a student starts out with the wrong heart in the whole learning process, they will themselves feel like they are unteachable. Now the young students are subjected to those kinds of worries. Now they have to overcome learning disabilities (and this certainly rang true).

I later asked God, "Why did I not understand what was being taught? Why was it so hard for me to get it?"

He actually answered, "I wanted to teach you. Not the ways of man and their traditional ways."

Wow! That made me feel better about myself. He showed me years later that I can be and learn all things through Christ. Do you realize how cool that information was to me? It was liberation. Where there is Jesus Christ, there is liberty. Oh, this is powerful good news! But I didn't ask this question for many years to come.

CHAPTER 12

The Nasal Voice

I was asked once in my short, young career in elementary school to get up in front of the class and give a speech.

"*What?*"

Being young and very creative, I racked my brain on how to get out of this. I thought, *I will change my voice where absolutely no one will want to hear me.* One very nasal voice flowed out of me like a river. One nasal voice coming up! By doing this, I created a huge problem. This change altered my life, but I wasn't thinking about the long road, of course. I just wanted no one literally to ever want me to give a speech again. With that plan hatched, I self-inflicted a speech pediment for most of my childhood. I literally trained myself so well that I couldn't stop even if I wanted to. Well, that did not go as planned. My reward: I was awarded a speech therapist for years. Hmmm. I am brilliant!

There was one good thing out of all this: a single individually wrapped peanut butter indulgence for the sweet tooth in me. I would get just one if I did everything right in speech class. Now that was pure motivation for that sweet tooth. However great that was, now came the labels, as dumb and unreachable, and my maiden name did not help either—River. My father had a military career and loved to live by a river whenever we moved. Go figure—last name River, and we lived by a river. You guessed it, weirdo. You know how cruel kids can be. Right? Not to mention the bullying that came with that name from the kids at school.

The sad thing is the student (me) started to believe the lie. All along, it was the child with fear who needed to overcome the problem, and I knew exactly how I got there in the first place, and the teachers . . . Well, they really don't have that much time on their hands. To figure out all this was a big mistake in the brain of a young child who did not want to speak in front of the class. The kids in school can be literally cruel. Does this sound familiar? Not sure if any of you have a story of your own to insert here. But this is what happened to me. Even at home, during my homework, if I asked for help, I felt rejected, and I never measured up to my elder brothers' and sisters' abilities. So I stopped asking.

No one should have to feel this way. For heaven's sake, I was just a child trying to learn. I did learn from these mistakes and did vow to be sensitive to the needs of mistreated children. God is just the opposite of failure. He can use failure to His glory! So try not to be so hard on yourself. This is fabulous news, really, really great news. He uses failure to bring glory back to himself. Wow! He makes us strong in our weakness. He helps us overcome any and all failures. He really has a love for us to learn. Learning is fun! The mystery of the whole universe is in His hands, and He wants to share it with us. How glorious!

> Call unto me, and I will answer thee and show thee great
> and mighty things which thou knowest not. (Jeremiah 33:3 KJV)

He is the greatest, the most everlasting love. The Father has such an amazing sense of humor that has no end, and His teaching abilities—well, they are endless. He is perfect love, and the scriptures tell me that He is where love originates.

CHAPTER 13

The Greatest Gift

We all want to be loved. That is the bottom line. We are not designed to be alone. When I was a young girl, I would collect cartoon drawings of what love is and plaster my bedroom walls with thousands of these. Love is . . . whatever the cartoon said it was.

Talking about love is cheap. Showing others what love is through action is the greatest way to love. Without love, we have nothing. Love is the greatest commandment. Why? The Lord said if we love, everything else will take care of itself because love is what we put out to be able to experience it here on the earth. You may not feel loved, but the great news is you are loved. You are loved with a passion. Tell yourself right now that you are loved with a passion, for Christ knows us from the very depths of our being. Yet many do not experience this love. This love is there when you don't feel it. This love holds you in your dark moments, hoping you find one who may help you understand what is happening in your heart. This love has the greatest power for freedom from yourself. This love is perfect even when things aren't.

This love will stay in your heart. This love will never leave you. The heart will love. It is real. This love will melt everything away except you and the Designer of love. We have to be open to surrounding ourselves with the positive words of love. Love really is all around us—the fresh air, the waterfalls, the simple pleasure of the soft green grass, the kiss of a puppy, the scent of the flowers, the beauty of the butterfly, the strength of a loin, the wonder of the birth of a child. Oh my—love! We have so much to be thankful for. We just have to hear it with the heart, see it with the soul, and know that we know and not lean on our own understanding. It surrounds us.

But I really didn't quite get this concept as a young lady. Why? Because I did not have a personal relationship with the Creator of love. It makes a lot of difference. Really! I knew love is profoundly tender and affectionate. My mother and my childhood flooded me with warmth and a personal attachment of love that I remember thinking I could never live without her or my family.

CHAPTER 14

The Garden of Gethsemane

Christ's affectionate concern for the well-being of others caused Him to lay down His life, His strength, His comfort, His pleasure for us all. But some never get it. I know one fact about love, and this may surprise you—love hurts.

Jesus was the perfect sacrifice of love, praised by those who believed in Him. He suffered a great deal. He asked His Father for the cup to pass Him because He knew what was being asked of Him. The stress of it all caused the capillaries to burst, and He began to sweat blood.

You might ask me, "How do you have knowledge of this?" Well, it all started in the church that had stained-glass windows. Not long ago, I needed to be with the Lord. What better place to go? I needed to go and sit under the stained glass of the Garden of Gethsemane. As I sat praying and singing between the pews on the floor, the Lord gave a vision of the stress He had been under. He knew He needed to be with His Father. He felt the pain long before He had actually gone through the physical act of the greatest love offered to mankind, and He knew He had to do it and fix things once and for all—and He did.

I got so wrapped up in my time and worship with the Lord that I almost got locked into the church for the night. I must have been there for hours. I caught a glimpse out one of the windows and realized it was dark. Oops!

CHAPTER 15

People Want Realness

In 1 Corinthians 1–13, Paul tells the people that if he entered a church, he would rather hear someone speak the language of the area than hear people speak in tongues. Why? How is someone going to get any value in hearing the unknown tongue, especially if you don't understand what is going on around you? Of course, believers know that this is your heavenly language that goes straight to the throne road of God, and Satan can't interpret what is being said. Paul tells us that a person who is not in tune with the Spirit of God, which is a gift, cannot understand the mystery of the Spiritual tongue. But have no fear, for the Lord would desire for you to understand. You must ask Him. So Satan can't understand, for it is a gift from the Father, and Satan was thrown from grace. This tongue is a secret weapon that Satan can't intercept.

You can read more in 1 Corinthians 2:14. This will confuse all with the lack of understanding and discernment. It applies to all unbelievers. Satan knows there is a God, and he believes probably more than us. But he was banished from everlasting love in the presence of the true living God. He messed up in his *vain* thinking. He was the most beautiful creature. It went to his head, and he tried taking others with him—and Satan wants you. His followers, the demons, fell with him.

Speech in tongues is one of the many protection forces from evil. It causes utter confusion. Paul mentions that he does speak in tongues and probably more than most. But basically, there is a time and a place for it. But in it all, Christ brings everything back to *love*.

Though I speak with the tongues of men and of angels but have not love, I have become a sounding brass or a clanging cymbal. Though I have the gift of prophecy and understand all mysteries and all knowledge and though I have faith so that I could move mountains, with no love, I am nothing. Though I bestow all my goods to feed the poor and though I give my body to be burned, with no love, it does not benefit me.

Love suffers long and is kind. Love does not envy. Love does not parade itself, is not puffed up, does not behave rudely, does not seek its own, is not provoked, thinks no evil, does not rejoice in iniquity but rejoices in the truth, bears all things, believes all things, hopes all things, endures all things. Love never fails. But whether there are prophecies, they will fail. Whether there are tongues, they will cease. Whether there is knowledge, it will vanish, for we know in part, and we prophesy in part. But when that which is perfect has come, that which is in part will be done.

When I was a child, I spoke as a child. I understood as a child. I thought as a child. But when I became a man, I put away childish things. For now, we see in a mirror dimly but then face-to-face. Now I know in part, but then I shall know just as I also am known. He knows us personally (everything), all the hidden sins and shame we know we have, yet He loves. How *great* is this news? Great, I tell you—great! Now abide faith, hope, love, these three—but the greatest of these is love.

> Anyone who does not love does not know God because God is love. (1 John 4:8 ESV)

Love takes the confessed sins and throws them into the sea, never to be reminded of again. We as Christians need to offer answers to those who are looking, not fakeness. Get to know people. Really know them. That is what counts. Don't let them come in looking for answers and walk away without them. Feel them up.

CHAPTER 16

Search Deep Within

One thing that I have learned is that God has a great sense of humor, and He is not oppressive. He accepts us as we are. (But I promise you you will want to change.) He's full of joy. He is humorous. He is perfect. He is a perfect gentleman. He is a lover. Forget that. He is the master lover. Oh, hallelujah! Praise Him! In return, we turn from what is not of Him and desire to know Him more and more through this powerful love that a lot of us don't fully understand. Oh, praise Him! He is perfect in every sense of the word, and His love for us goes beyond the realm of what we know or can comprehend.

Somewhere deep within me, something was drawing me to want to know more. But where and how can I begin to even understand this God who lives and loves so highly in the fullness of goodness? My innermost being is whispering to me. *But how? How, God?* In uncertainties in life, I needed more. I certainly didn't know my future, but God did, and some of it can be painful, and in that, I would search even deeper. Does that make sense?

God, I know you are real with the stories found in your Bible. I find myself caught up with you. How does one come to you in an approachable and tangible way? Is it looking up to the heavens to pray, bowing my head in awe of you, and taking in your beauty? The very air I breathe comes from you, I know. How, oh, how do I find you? I am having the hopes that you would hear and see this speck of life from your throne. This is my perception of you. But in this youth, I searched for you. I did not have a personal relationship with you. In fact, I really did not think I could know you up close and personal, even call you my friend. But for some reason, you were the one I would turn to in my many years of on-and-off tears. You were there but only in an invisible way. I know because I talked with you. But are you really real?

Chapter 17

My Early Perception

I know you are looking down from your throne and watching us, and if we mess up, you will be punishing us, and we will go to a place that is never-ending flames—if we are lucky (I don't use the word *luck* in my vocabulary). The word *luck* gives credit to something else other than God. He is the giver, not luck. Luck had nothing to do with it. Christians generally believe in the sovereignty of God, and His plan is at work, and His gifts happen to all of us for a reason, whatever that reason might be, not luck.

With all that said on luck, my thoughts that the church taught me or what I thought they were teaching me was that a person would go to a holding tank, and family members alive on earth could pray you out. That is if you died and did not get to be in the presence of God, in the paradise that was lost from not understanding and truly knowing you as our personal Father—in other words, having no assurance, just merely hoping. And guess what? This is actually where I was. I had no real assurance. At least, that is what I thought.

The holding tank is actually found in the scriptures, and it is probably the scriptures that are being used to say that you can get prayed out of purgatory. Nope. That was only good for the Old Testament saints, and they did get delivered out of a holding tank. They knew that God was going to send a son to rescue them. It was foretold.

CHAPTER 18

David Is Rescued from the Holding Tank

David and the saints were in that holding place, and Jesus saved them. David knew this and talked about it years before the arrival of Jesus and in the realm of His death. It was finished at the last breath, the death of His majesty, His crucifixion at the cross. He took all the sins of the world to free us who believe, descending to hell to free the captives from purgatory. What a glorious day! I can only imagine the scene.

Jesus suddenly appeared at the gates of hell. His brightness shone with absolute assuredness. Nothing absolutely nothing stops Him from ripping down the doors that hold His beloved saints, the intense blaze of passion that He is assuring in the underworld, the power of God being unleashed within the darkness, the light of His glory penetrating and killing the destructive power that kills, steals, and destroys, shattering Satan's hope of separating the saints from the King. Jesus brought salvation, redemption, and fulfillment of the promises to the ones who foretold of this day long ago. The righteous are saved. What a glorious day indeed!

Oh, the splendor, the colors of all the precious jewels showering beams down through the darkness in every direction, the illumination of the lights captivating the presence of the Lord's pure holiness and truth forevermore! The heavenly body of the Holy One's Spirit now saturated the whole place with glory. Stand down and watch the King of Kings take what belongs to Him for His glory. Yes, He fights our battles. His promises are "Yes" and "Amen."

David was a mighty warrior, and he understood authorities and principality. He knew that this day would come. Can you imagine the praise that carried on in that holding place? Oh, what a welcome! What a marvelous sight to behold! David, Abraham, Isaac, Jacob, John the Baptist, and all the saints of the Old Testament—the hearts are joined as one as they hear the beating of the Lord's heart of love for them. Perfect—they are in perfect beauty. It is surrounding them.

Oh, how God has answered their prayers! Their hearts were filled and became as one. What a miracle! We knew this day would come. God surely knew what He was doing. His beauty blinds Satan as he comes in to rescue the hearts that are now reflected in the eyes of the saints. You are the most beautiful creation in the whole of eternity. I love you more than words could ever find or say. This is a perfect piece of art. You freed us from the depths of the darkness, like the rose in its fullness of beauty, the love of our everlasting God, who all knows and protects us.

> For great is thy mercy toward me, and thou hast delivered my soul from the lowest hell. (Psalms 86:13 KJV)
> After His resurrection, Jesus ascends to heaven and brings the ransomed dead with Him so that now paradise is no longer down near the place of torment but is up in the third heaven, the highest heaven, where God dwells! (2 Corinthians 12:2–4)

Oh my gosh. Did you just hear that? "So now paradise is no longer down near the place of torment." He has made every provision. We are without excuse.

> There was a certain rich man who was clothed in purple and fine linen and fared sumptuously every day. And there was a certain beggar named Lazarus who was laid at his gate, full of sores, desiring to be fed with the crumbs which fell from the rich man's table. Moreover, the dogs came and licked his sores. And it came to pass that the beggar died and was carried by the angels into Abraham's bosom. The rich man also died and was buried. And in hell, he lift up his eyes, being in torment, and seeth Abraham afar off and Lazarus in his bosom. And he cried and said, "Father Abraham, have mercy on me and send Lazarus, that he may dip the tip of his finger in water and cool my tongue, for I am tormented in this flame." But Abraham said, "Son, remember that thou in thy lifetime received thy good things, and likewise, Lazarus evil things, but now he is comforted, and thou art tormented. And beside all this, between us and you, there is a great gulf fixed so that they which would pass from hence to you cannot. Neither can they pass to us that would come from thence." Then he said, "I pray thee therefore, Father, that thou wouldest send him to my father's house. For I have five brethren, that he may testify unto them, lest they also come into this place of torment." Abraham saith unto him, "They have Moses and the prophets. Let them hear them." And he said, "Nay, Father Abraham, but if one went unto them from

the dead, they will repent." And he said unto him, "If they hear not Moses and the prophets, neither will they be persuaded, though one rose from the dead." (Luke 16:19–31 KJV)

Now the church, those in Christ Jesus, the righteous, pass. They aren't merely carried by angels to Abraham's bosom. They go to be with Christ, which is far better than before Christ and what those who died had to go through. This is found in Philippians 1:23. Please read it for yourself.

> The wicked, however, remain in Hades in torment until the final judgment, when Hades gives up the dead who dwell there, and they are judged according to their deeds, and then Death and Hades are thrown into hell, into the lake of fire. (Revelation 20:13–15)

It's there in black and white. Please read it for yourself. But why wait? We are given an allotted time. I believe that a seed is given to everyone at conception. The heart and Spirit grows in either direction as we are loved or not loved. It's sad to say, but others do form us and our beliefs at times. Some experience only rejection and are mistreated by others. This rejection is hard to overcome. But great news: it can be overcome. Let go.

But that is the beauty of Jesus. We get to choose and forgive. Be happy, whether you feel it or not. Pray for those who misuse us. Can you imagine being beaten, spit on, nailed, tortured, called names, mocked? (If you are the God you say you are, then save yourself. Show us basically. Thrill us basically. My thoughts on that: *Hello, were you not listening or watching all the miracles He did for us? Are you serious right now?*)

Having a humble heart and staying busy and choosing to trust is a great place to be. Christ never chose certain situations for you. Others did by the way they treated you, good or bad. But this is great news. Why? Because Christ freed us from that curse, for He has overcome the world and the evil within its atmosphere. We are grafted in. Oh, hallelujah!

> Let your conversation be without covetousness, and be content with such things as ye have, for he hath said, "I will never leave thee nor forsake thee." (Hebrews 13:5 KJV)

This is absolutely one of my favorite verses, for no matter what I am going through, He is with me. It's only time after time if we reject His unfailing love and then take our last breath on Earth that we will know we missed it. Oh my! What a horrible situation to be in when He gave so much to us! We were appointed a time to live and love and a time to die. Unfortunately, those who never knew Him really never knew Him, even "once saved, always saved" Christians. We all need to look at ourselves and love the way Christ loved. He loves the lost, the sick, the homeless, the less fortunate, the ones who have no hope.

Let us say as the scriptures say. Those who are whole are in no need for a doctor. Jesus did not come for the righteous and prideful, but He came to help the ones who know that they are sick and realize they need to repent. They realize they are not perfect, and that is a beautiful place to be. You should *never* put yourself above someone else. This *will* cause one to be separated forever. Satan wins. When our Spirit comes to life in Christ, we want to share the amazing news.

> But let us, who are of the day, be sober, putting on the breastplate of faith and love and, for a helmet, the hope of salvation. For God hath not appointed us to wrath but to obtain salvation by our Lord Jesus Christ, who died for us, that whether we wake or sleep, we should live together with him. Wherefore comfort yourselves together and edify one another. (1 Thessalonians 5:8–11 KJV)

I have learned that you keep us even when we don't know it. You, Father, are special in every sense of the word. You have the ultimate spiritual peace, and your purpose is to help us free ourselves from ourselves and connect to something bigger than ourselves.

CHAPTER 19

Traditions Are Like Clockwork

Meanwhile, as I was thinking these things, I did not escape the church. (Thank you, Mom!) My mother had us in church every Sunday, and we had catechism every week. Yet I always knew when church was almost over because I was so programmed that when I pulled my elastic hairband back to reset the few loose strands of flyaway hairs, sure enough, just like that, like clockwork, church was over. Everyone filed out in a rush from the cathedral, only to live their lives as they saw fit.

I recalled that many were hardly well out the door and were lighting up a cigarette, and I wondered about that. I even questioned my own life and the lives of my family, who were not perfect. We told lies, but who doesn't? We are all guilty. As a whole, we were not really spiritual. Really, we had issues. Yet on Sunday, we were different for one hour. We were . . . holier? Hmmm . . . I did wonder. In it all, I felt like I was special, and I got the big prize. I was going to heaven—heaven bound, according to the teachings of being baptized as a baby. That's really not how it works either. I was really just dedicated to the Lord. Real baptism will come much later in my life—many years later, that is. Amen!

Chapter 20

Abigail's First Encounter

Abigail is Hebrew and means, "My Father is joyful." Abigail also means, "She knows." God is pure perfection, and we will find beauty in trusting Him, but we must trust Him even when things go wrong. He turns the very thing that is evil into something beautiful. This is certainly interesting. Many years before the birth of Abigail, God knew her, formed her, and told her that something beautiful will happen in her life—when she literally felt like she had no hope.

I, Abigail, had the first of many encounters, knowing that I was not the only one in the room, especially when I was the only one in the room—or so I thought. I heard a voice from a mysterious, nonexistent reality (as one would know it). A voice called out my name as I stood in my parents' hallway next to the bathroom opening.

Softly, it said, "Abigail."

I did not recognize this voice, yet it was real, and it was calling my name. I froze with sudden fear, turning my head where I heard the voice. I stood clutching my nightgown. Time seemed to stand still. My heart, pounding in my chest, felt like it was about to burst. The whole atmosphere around me became so alive that I could hear the air breathing.

This certainly gave me great apprehension of my own physical realm of reality, knowing that there were creative powers beyond what I understood, good or bad, but which one is it? (Actually, I did not care to know.) I did have peace, but it was frightening (if that makes sense). I did believe quietly in my heart that it was good. I knew that God existed, I just couldn't see anything, and I really did not want to see. But there had to be a supernatural side to this, and I did not understand. I had never expected a personal encounter. This encounter constituted a realness in my nervousness, and I went on and on thinking and rethinking, rehashing what had happened, thinking over and over. This was distinguishable and altogether most definitely not normal by any means to the world that I knew. *What is this?* I wondered.

Assuring myself, I knew in my heart of hearts that it was a special superpower, a peaceable power—or was it? I was second-guessing myself. It was a power greater in the scope and magnitude of reality. But I certainly considered it not natural to me or something that had ever previously existed in my life. A supernatural world of which I knew nothing—was it a trick? Was it something appearing as kind and yet in reality was something very bad?

I was so shaken. I was unable to free myself—my heart, mind, body, and spirit. This emotional experience was so frightening, and whatever it was, it was trying to have contact with me. My heart leapt with distressing emotions and was aroused. What possible impending danger, evil, or pain could be lurking? I was so unsure of whether the threat was real or imagined. This feeling conditioned me to being afraid, and it was awful, to say the least. I was so young and innocent, and I could not tell anyone for fear they would lock me up.

Yet why did I have the feeling of peace, a reverential awe, especially toward God, and the fear of Him all at the same time? Why was this something causing me feelings of dread or apprehension? (Looking back now, I can honestly say the fear was the unknown.) Is this . . . something to be afraid of? *What is it?* I knew something was present, foreign, and unexpected. But as I was thinking these thoughts, whatever it was, I noticed that it was like a gentleman because every time I closed my eyes and asked for it to go, it would leave. I figured if it was bad, it would not leave me. It would torture me. Right? Not fun.

I did not understand the wholeness of God, and I certainly did not know any scriptures. In fact, we were not encouraged to read our Bible. The priest told us what we needed to know. I guess. At least, that was my perception. Yet years went by, and slowly, God was revealing His realness to me. With each rotation of the earth, He was there, every nanosecond, minute, day, week, month, and year. It certainly was and is His choice, but one thing is for sure—He's holding it all together. This seems so elementary—the earth, the sun—yet it isn't. It is so complex and detailed to the very last drop. In fact, there is no end. We are only allowed to see what is physical (yet others see the mysterious ways too), but it is so much bigger than that.

He asks us to call on Him, and when we do, He says, "I will answer you." Not only will He answer you, but also, He will show you things that we know not. How cool is that? This word is found in Jeremiah 33:3. Take note of the three threes. That is triple communication. His words are deep, deeper than we can imagine, and He works in threes. Three is communication. He does have triple communication with us. Are we really listening? The Father, the Son, and the Holy Ghost—what actually are we surrendering to?

You own it all, Jesus. He has given us all freedom to decide, but I promise when you do give it all back with gratitude, you will find a peace that you never understood. There is a wonderful working power, power, power, power in the name of Jesus. What do you have to give up? A heart of stone? Roads with twists and turns? I promise, you really have nothing without Him!

His heavenly angels sing, "Holy, holy, holy is the Lord God Almighty. Sweet smells of fragrance are around His throne." Come join them and feel the presence of the living God Almighty. Let's join in one accord, for He has asked us to do, and it is possible with the Holy Spirit. He has given everything you need.

Oh my! Early life—how it was in vain. We must put the past behind us. As children, we longed for Superman or Spider-Man or all the superheroes to rescue the good from evil. That is Jesus. He is the superhero. "I Am" is a jealous God. "I Am" is yours. Are you His? We have been deceived. Please bring His glorious name back to life in your heart and mind and free yourself from themselves through Christ. Oh, how He loves you! Do you hear Him? "I love *you!*"

The earth and the fullness thereof is His. Think on this concept alone. Earth's path goes around the sun. We call this an orbit. It takes the earth 365¼ days (one year) to complete the orbit. As the earth orbits the sun, the moon orbits the earth, and with all things happening, this causes the ocean waters to create high and low tides. Who can fathom the seriousness of just this one concept, His creation, His gift to us, our inheritance by the master engineer and artist, His grace? I was becoming a student of His. Amen! I have so much to learn.

CHAPTER 21

He Is a Jealous God

But the scriptures clearly talk about the heart in many different, wonderful ways, and a lot is pure good—yet there is one that stood out as very strange to me.

> The heart is deceitful above all things, and it is exceedingly corrupt. Who can know it? I, Jehovah, search the mind. I try the heart, even to give every man according to his ways, according to the fruit of his doings. As the partridge that sitteth on eggs which she hath not laid, so is he that getteth riches and not by right. In the midst of his days, they shall leave him, and at his end, he shall be a fool. A glorious throne, set on high from the beginning, is the place of our sanctuary. (Jeremiah 17:9–12 ASV)

I believe what he is saying is that it is not the heart we should trust or the basket that holds our eggs that matter. It is the throne of the Living God, for it is He who gives, gave, and will give to us all. His gifts are the birth, the life, the death. The glorious throne is set in the highest of places from which all things have their beginning. He gets the glory, not things. Our heart is a thing that He gave. How can we take credit? He made it.

In other words, we are all sitting on His eggs and the things that go in "the basket." They are *all* His as well. We really did not lay them or make them. We receive riches that we cannot take credit for, and we will leave them all one day. If we take the credit, we are fools. The heart will take credit and deceive us. Deep within each one of us is the gift. Search, and you will find. For he who believes in Jesus, rivers of living water will flow. It is found in the very depths of our bellies. This is a promise made to those who believe.

This encounter proves to be the beginning of a very serious moment for me, to say the least. I was so afraid and really didn't understand what was happening. I denied it. I pushed it away, and when I pushed, it left me, giving me hope to believe that it was on the good side. Besides, if it weren't, wouldn't it want to torture me and not leave? Right? As I once said before, I wanted to deny the whole experience. But with each thought, the more I tried to deny it happened, the more I knew it was real. I really refused to even think about it, let alone talk about it.

> Blessed be the God and Father of our Lord Jesus Christ, who hath blessed us with every spiritual blessing in the heavenly places in Christ, even as he chose us in him before the foundation of the world, that we should be holy and without blemish before him in love, having foreordained us unto adoption as sons and daughters through Jesus Christ unto himself, according to the good pleasure of his will, to the praise of the glory of his grace, which he freely bestowed on us in the Beloved, in whom we have our redemption through his blood, the forgiveness of our trespasses, according to the riches of his grace, which he made to abound toward us in all wisdom and prudence, making known unto us the mystery of his will, according to his good pleasure which he purposed in him unto a dispensation of the fullness of the times, to sum up all things in Christ, the things in the heavens, and the things upon the earth, in him, I say, in whom also we were made a heritage, having been foreordained according to the purpose of him who worketh all things after the counsel of his will, to the end that we should be unto the praise of his glory, we who had before hoped in Christ, in whom ye also, having heard the word of the truth, the gospel of your salvation, in whom, having also believed, ye were sealed with the Holy Spirit of promise, which is an earnest of our inheritance, unto the redemption of God's own possession, unto the praise of his glory. For this cause, I also, having heard of the faith in the Lord Jesus which is among you and the love which ye show toward all the saints. (Ephesians 1:3–15 ASV)

Well, so much is said to us in the scriptures. It is important to know the scriptures. If we never read the Holy Book, we will never know. Surrendering to God the Father, Son, and Holy Ghost will open a new world to you, and you can get the fullness of the writings. Understanding this will give you a purpose. It is a mystery, yet He is willing to give the mystery to His glory. To be able to understand His inheritance from us, we share His amazing love that knew us even before the foundation of the earth.

I am in the process of finding refuge under His wings, and I did not know. Wow! My sheep know my voice. I didn't know Him yet, but He certainly and clearly knows me, just as He knows you. ♥ I was being introduced to the Most High God and His army of angels, which we all have access to. Peter said God does not have a favorite. What He has done for one, He will do for another. We should, however, have a reverence for the Creator, that through Him, He has worked and will work out the righteousness that is acceptable to the Father. Oh my goodness—this is amazing news! (Acts 10:34–35)

> For there is no respect of persons with God. For as many as have sinned without the law shall also perish without the law. and as many as have sinned under the law shall be judged by the law, for not the hearers of the law are just before God, but the doers of the law shall be justified (for when Gentiles that have not the law do by nature the things of the law, these, not having the law, are the law unto themselves in that they show the work of the law written in their hearts, their consciences bearing witness therewith, and their thoughts one with another accusing or else excusing them) in the day when God shall judge the secrets of men, according to my gospel, by Jesus Christ. (Romans 2:11–16 ASV)

The law condemns us, but Jesus came to free us from the law. The people were using works rather than love. We are walking in His supreme presence, with shelter that some are not aware of, like I was, yet He was there, protecting, and if you don't see it or feel it, trust me, it is there right here, right now. The fullness of knowing it can get blocked by the enemy because of the curse that fell and continues to fall on the earth. This is the whole reason Jesus came—so that He can free us from the curse. That is an amazing Father!

CHAPTER 22

Great News!

My sheep hear my voice, and I know them, and they follow me. And I give unto them eternal life, and they shall never perish. Neither shall any man pluck them out of my hand. (John 10:27–28 KJV)

> And Jesus, answering, said unto them, "They that are in health have no need of a physician but they that are sick. I am not coming to call the righteous but sinners to repentance." (Luke 5:31–32 ASV)

This is great news. You don't have to be perfect. Those who think they are miss it! He came to save the sick, the sinners without hope. He loves you. He calls. Even before the foundations of the earth, He knew us. He is calling us whether we realize it or not. We will not be without an excuse.

His son Jesus took it all for us to free us once and for all from the father of lies, Satan. The religious ones created traditional ways, making themselves the focus and belittling others whom they thought could never measure up. (Jesus had to save us from man too.) Well, guess what? We will never measure up. We can't. It is not by our works that we are saved. Yes, faith without works is dead. But the work that we do should all go back to the Father, who gave us the will to choose. He wants you—a surrendering heart. If we give it all back to Him, He receives the glory for redeeming us from Satan, and manmade works and holding onto traditions are Satan's plan, not God's. All along, it was God who gave us the original garden to be free to walk with Him and have communication. Satan has to have truth mix with the lie. Without truth, you will not believe the lie. It is through the flesh that was ripped from His bones that He healed us from all sickness and disease. It is a gift that He gives to show His unfailing love toward us. ♥

CHAPTER 23

The Lambs' Book of Life

"For I know the thoughts that I think toward you," saith the Lord, "thoughts of peace and not of evil, to give you an expected end." (Jeremiah 29:11 KJV)

How great is our God? Please take a moment and ponder this question. He has planned an expected end. You have to choose the path.

I like to look at it this way. We have three books in heaven. (Hmmm . . . three again . . . The Father, the Son, the Holy Ghost.) Book one is filled with all the names of people who have ever existed, even the stillborn and the aborted. The unborn who existed in the womb are immediately carried to be in the presence of the Lord God Almighty. The children are taught to forgive the parents who took their lives by Jesus himself, the master forgiver. If you are one of these parents, please forgive yourself and give your child a name, one if it were a boy or if it were a girl. They have forgiven you. Jesus came to save you and love you like no other and gave the chance to know the real God as you live on the earth. If we never make the choice to know the power that frees us in Jesus, we are blotted out.

Revelation 17:8 talks about the beast who was and became of not yet is very much real. He makes his final appearance from the bottomless pit to the spiritual ruin of the loss and the damnation of whom he can take with him. Why does he do this? To go before the King (the lawyer, the one who stood in the gap). Satan wants to make a case against you. He is the accuser. Jesus is the ultimate gift giver. Have you believed and asked forgiveness of your sins? He is waiting. You will not be blotted out if your confession is to Jesus and you turn from your wrongs, never to be reminded of them again. This is great news. No matter how bad you are, God loves you. This is Satan's loss, and he wants you to think what I am saying is a bunch of hogwash. Please don't let this be your future state of the all the wicked who are utterly fallen to destruction.

You may say, "Well, that certainly doesn't apply to me. I am not really wicked." However, if you think you can do this on your own when there was the Creator, who conquered the grave. That's not good because we can't do it on our own. That's exactly what Satan thought. "I don't need God. I'm better, I'm bigger, I'm greater, and I'm perfect to look at in all my glory. Just look at me, look at me, look at me!" And where did it get him?

There comes a time that we are all going to give an account. When we live, we have grace. You may say, "I am good. I never murdered anyone." Hmmm Even a murderer can be deem saved through the blood and resurrected through Christ. I promise you this. You will wonder at the end of time, *Is my name in the book, or am I blotted out?* Or you could be the one standing there, saying, "Oh my! There's a God, and I missed it." I have utter failure of pure separation from the Creator. You can have assurance that you will not be blotted out by realizing this all before you are called out of this life. Don't let anyone steal your joy, not even you. Let go. You really don't own your life anyways. You were bought with a price.

Many times, temptation is put before us, and why is that? To see if we truly pass the test, and sometimes we don't. God wants the heart and for you to decide. He is a perfect gentleman. He will force nothing on you. Why? Freedom lets you decide. But if you make the wrong choice, we will feel it somewhere down the road. If we fail, which we do sometimes, we can ask forgiveness, but if we resort to doing wrong and asking forgiveness later, well, we have failed big time. That is the wrong thought process. I have a perfect example of temptation. Let's say you see something as simple as a comb, and you think, *I will just pick it up and take it home.* Before you take it, remember that the comb will cry out to God and say, "I am not where I belong." Would you still want it, knowing that it talks to God? I think not because now there is an account of where it is. It will not be hidden. The truth will come out, and don't think that it will not. There—the problem is solved. You have overcome it because that is what happens to objects that are stolen—they cry out. Revelation 3:5 says if we overcome the temptation . . . How do you overcome this? Thinking about the Creator helps when making choices! His will is that we be presented to Him, and seeing that Jesus is the only way, He will not blot your name out. He will confess to you before His Father and His angels!

Three in Revelation is the communication, and five is the grace received (Revelation 3:5). We are given every opportunity to receive. Listen closely to all that is around you. Really hear. Try it. Then ask yourself, *Do I receive the truth that is all around me?* If you do, then ask Him in—if you haven't already. You only have to lose Satan. Ha! You may be asking how I overcame it all. I am a human. I know my dirty deeds. Yes, and He knows them better than yourself. You may have forgotten some. Hmmm . . . You can put it to rest once and for all through Jesus.

Book two is God's perfect plan for your life that is covered by His son's blood. When God the Father looks at you, He sees His precious Son's blood. It covers you and washes you white as snow. How glorious! Jesus is our lawyer when the accuser comes in the presence of the Lord to condemn us. The lambs' book of life is opened, and your name is not blotted out, for you know and love Jesus and what He has done for you at the cross. In Jeremiah 29:11, Jesus has good thoughts of you, and He wants to give you peace and hope. He understands the evil that is present in this world. This is why He desires for you to understand—so He won't have separation from you.

Book three is the book of lies, the road God never planned for your life, the life you chose without the Son Jesus. Sad, sad, sad! It is for a good understanding that clearly, we are warned. If we are not careful and clearly do not understand that we are placed by the Master, He puts us in certain situations. We might become rich. We may be teachers. We may become famous preachers. The list goes on and on of the endless possibilities for one's life. But who placed us there through the heart of the willingness to want in the first place? Hmmm. I am going to say God. That's who. But in the riches, we become full of ourselves and miss it. It becomes a self-inflicted wound!

Saul was a nobody, and God made him somebody, and in his richness, he lost himself and was stripped from his glory and died. Nebuchadnezzar was another man who brought destruction upon himself for seven years, lost his mind, and lived like a wild animal—until one day he confessed who his Creator was and asked forgiveness. He was instantly healed, and God restored him. He, in return, gave back to God all the glory, and the whole nation worshipped the God of heaven. It became a living testimony for the nation to see.

CHAPTER 24

Food for Thought

Beware of the so-called people of God who are really wolves. You can certainly tell if one is of God by the way they talk and act. Do they talk about others behind their backs and say, "Oh, let me tell you something, but you promise not to say anything. Later, we can pray for them"? Huh? Excuse me? "God knows the details. Let's just pray for them." You've got to cut it off. Why? Because you are gossiping. I would not want anyone to know my business unless I share it with them. I think the Lord might call them a wolf.

A good standard for thought is if they are willing to spill the beans to me about another's personal life. Well, they will certainly spill the beans on yours and then say, "Let's pray." Really? I will not share even for prayer. You will recognize them by their fruits. So every healthy tree will bear good fruit, but the diseased tree needs to be chopped down, and if you live in the sticks like me, you will burn it to get rid of it. It is just that simple. That is what we do to a tree that does not bear good fruit. We should certainly think a Perfect Creator would do the same.

Satan is the one we should find fault with, not God. Satan is a deceiver. He wants you to do what you think is good for you and your happiness. The problem? Satan can't offer you anything except deception. God wants to give you the best. Well, if this is the God that is so perfect, why would He allow such destruction with gossip and choices? That's just it. He doesn't. We are free to do what we want.

We are not perfect, and the only way we can be forgiven is through the Son. Satan tricked Eve, and Adam blamed Eve. But Adam should have known better. They had the perfect setup. Perfect. This conversation could go on and on with explanation, and the answers are presented to those who want to know the truth, and it will set you free. It is finished.

CHAPTER 25

The Blame Game

Satan is the blame game. He has to find fault, and he loves gossip. Don't do it. It hurts those around us. The church is filled with it. Stop it, and if someone enters a church building, obviously, they are looking for answers, and they may be doodling or get distracted with a phone. Let them be because their ears are hearing the Word of God, which is a seed that was planted, which can grow in their life at some point. But it will have a hard time to grow if word gets back to them that you dislike something they were doing in the church building, looking at their phone, doodling, and not paying attention. What are you doing by watching them? Are you paying attention? Then you have a need to share this with others in the church, what someone else might be doing. Really? Do you see how ridiculous that is? People doodle. Now that person may never set foot in the church again because of you not paying attention either. Stop it.

Some have the act of holiness but will deny Christ's power. Jesus has the power to give all perfect gifts, whatever that might be—the power to heal (2 Timothy 3:5). Please don't be guided by those who will lead you away from Jesus because you will get swallowed up (Isaiah 9:16).

For nothing will be impossible with God. (Luke 1:37 ESV)

We must believe this statement. Oh my gosh! Jesus is calling you to Him. He loves you with the greatest passion. He was stripped, beaten, and hung on the cross. He died and went to hell to free the ones who had gone before Him and, in all glory, shows Himself to Mary Magdalene and His disciples once again. But before He goes to be with the Father, He leaves us a gift: the Holy Spirit to lead, guide, and teach us. Wow, all for us, in hopes that we might find the true gift of life! Oh, what a good, gracious, loving friend and lover of all people's souls and spirits! You are *loved*. ❤

You are His. Please don't go astray. Ask Him into your heart. Tell Him you are a sinner and you want to be born again through His son, who suffered, died, and was buried and rose again on the third day so that we could live. He will do the rest when you get into His Word of truth found in the Bible.

Here's some food for thought. Please digest slowly. *Enjoy.* Since I have become born again, my relationship with Jesus grows daily and deeper. I often wonder about the scriptures that tell us to pray continually. I thought in my early walk that that is impossible. But then I am also reminded of the scriptures that nothing is impossible for those who are in Christ Jesus!

My point is that I love it when He talks with me, and I desire more and more time with Him. Praying without ceasing is possible. In everything, I give thanks, not so much for a bad situation but thankful for the answer that He will give so that I can find my way out of a bad situation and give Him the glory when the answer arrives. We are to do greater work than Him. I am not seeing it. Are you? So I am praying. In John 14:6, Jesus tells us that He is the way, the truth, and the life. No one can come to the Father except through Him (Jesus). As I walk and talk with Him, desiring more and more, the Word is helpful to put aside all the murmuring.

When Moses and Aaron set the Israelites free from a bondage of four hundred years, they were seeing many miracles right before their eyes. They were standing at the edge of the land for freedom, and a sea of water was blocking the way! They looked at Moses and began to complain.

"We were better off as slaves. At least we had food," they were murmuring to themselves (even though as slaves, they were fed sparingly).

They were babies needing to be bottle-fed, but Moses was on solid food. His thoughts were of the Lord's. He too heard the voice of the Lord helping him and teaching him as he went. Can you imagine leading a mass of people and seeing one miracle after the next, only to hear complaining from their lips, such hypocrisy and slanderous words from the heart? Ungrateful twits, I say! My goodness. Pharaoh's whole army was right behind them, shaking the earth with the wheels of the chariots as they tore through the earth in pursuit of the slaves. Still, they did not believe in the power of the Lord, yet complaining was found on their lips.

Moses heard from the Lord, and He struck the water with the rod and raised his hands to shut them up with the mighty power of the Lord as He froze the waters with His very breath. The massive body of water turned into a frozen wall. Can you imagine? Can you see and hear the voices of the Israelites? They stood in awe of the Great "I Am's" power. Finally, an exposed area, safe and dry, a passage to cross! Wow! Hello? That is cool! I would be in awe just over that for the rest of my life.

As soon as they're across, the horse and its rider entered the same passage to cross. The Lord allowed them to enter the dry land, and as soon as all the chariots were completely inside, the wall of water that was being held up by the breath of God collapsed in on them. It was such a joyous moment, and Moses wrote a song:

> *The horse and the rider cast into the sea*
> *We shall sing unto the Lord, for He has triumphed gloriously*
> *The horse and the rider thrown into the sea*
> *The Lord, my God, my strength, my shield, and now He is my victory*
> *I will sing unto the Lord, for he is triumphant gloriously*
> *The horse and the rider thrown into the sea*

Wow! Wow! Wow! They had manna from heaven, and quails by the hundreds just showed up and landed beside them, making the birds easy prey ("Eat me"). In fact, they basically were buried in meat. They had to eat their way out, and by the time it was over, they were sick of quail! He provided food and shoes that never wore out in the forty years in the desert. Can you imagine? All that and more happened, and still, they complained. Really? (1 Peter 2:1–25)

We must keep our hearts with all diligence, as Proverbs 4:23 reads, for out of it flows the living springs of life. Life is a heart issue, and we have to guard it. Scripture is like the very breath of God, teaching us, guiding us, correcting us to do all that we can and have the fullness of life. We can be ready and know that also in John 15:13, Jesus calls you His friend, and He did lay down His life for you. John 10:10 reminds us that Satan *enjoys* killing, stealing, and destroying. The thief is Satan. He steals every day. We mustn't give Him power to take from us, and I am not only talking about material things. We allow him to steal our very lives through pride.

But Christ, He came to restore what was stolen, to go beyond our own thoughts. Who would not want that? He broke the generational curses because we are grafted into Him now. The veil was torn. He came to give life, and we have it abundantly. Notice it says, "Give life," but if we have life already, why would He give life again? We already have it. Yes, we do have life through the birth of our mothers. But that life was born into sin because Adam messed it all up for us. So Jesus came to give life that is found in Him through the Spirit, breaking the curse. Why would you not love Him? So Jesus is the second Adam born from the Spirit? Yes—and amen! He broke the *curse*. The first Adam was cursed through sin, *death*.

CHAPTER 26

Does a Thief Come Through the Front Door?

Let me ask you a question. If someone was trying to enter your home through a locked back door or through a window, what would you think? Of course, you would know that something is terribly wrong and immediately know that the person trying to enter does not belong at your back door or a window. You would quickly realize that that person is a thief and up to no good.

Jesus sums it up with words we find in John 10:1: "He that enters not by the door but tries some other way is a thief and a robber!"

No one enters through the gates of heaven except through Jesus. He is the only way into heaven through the front gates, which, by the way, are twelve gates, one for each tribe, and each one is made of a single pearl. Wow! I bet they are absolutely beautiful, the best of the best. We can't enter any other way. It is not by our good works or our righteousness but by Jesus. He covers the multitude of sins. He conquered the grave and freed us once and for all. Jesus is the way, truth, and life. Amen. He is the great "I Am."

I was there in the beginning. I am . . . the Word, and the
Word was with God, and the Word was God. I am. (John 1:1)

CHAPTER 27

Your Words Have Power!

O God, mighty in all things, heaven is filled with your glory! You alone are worthy of all honors. You have given the ultimate price. You are a glorious king. You are the one who has provided everything. In you, we shall find our protection under your wings. Your asking price? You paid it all. Freedom—you gave it all. You became poor so that we can become rich, rich in love. Praise belongs to you! Even creation sings. The rocks cry out to you. The flowers sing. The air even has a vibration in harmony with you. Everything to the king!

What does your word say out of your mouth? For out of it are the issues of life. Being a mother, I remind my children of these words: "Be careful what you say." Jesus taught me this so long ago. Amen! You can bring good or bad. Which do you choose?

Back in the day, my neighbor's child would walk around his house, singing this strange song, "The Roof Is On Fire." He did this all the time.

One day I went to him, and I told him, "You need to stop singing that song. Why are you singing that song? That is a strange song to sing."

He said he just liked the sound of it and the beat.

"You really should not say those words, let alone sing them."

He said, "Why?"

I told him, "You will have what you say."

He chuckled, thinking I was crazy. Hmmm . . . Well, guess what? The day came, and the roof was on fire, just as he confessed in a song.

> The revelation of Jesus Christ, God gave him to show to his
> servants the things that must soon take place. He made it known
> by sending his angel to his servant John, who bore witness to
> the word of God and to the testimony of Jesus Christ, even to

all that he saw. Blessed is the one who reads aloud the words of this prophecy, and blessed are those who hear and who keep what is written. Grace to you and peace from him who is and who was and who is to come and from the seven spirits who are before his throne and from Jesus Christ, the faithful witness, the firstborn of the dead, and the ruler of kings on earth. To him who loves us and has freed us from our sins by his blood. (Revelation 1:1–20 ESV)

Can I get a hallelujah here?

Forsaking the right way, they have gone astray. (2 Peter 2:15 ESV)

CHAPTER 28

Veiled or Unveiled

Therefore, having this ministry by the mercy of God, we do not lose heart. But we have renounced disgraceful, underhanded ways. We refuse to practice cunning or to tamper with God's word, but by the open statement of the truth, we would commend ourselves to everyone's conscience in the sight of God. And even if our gospel is veiled, it is veiled only to those who are perishing. In their case, the god of this world has blinded the minds of the unbelievers, to keep them from seeing the light of the gospel of the glory of Christ, who is the image of God. For what we proclaim is not ourselves but Jesus Christ as Lord, with ourselves as your servants, for Jesus's sake. (2 Corinthians 4:1–18 ESV)

I mentioned earlier that the message Jesus sent was to stop the traditional ways of man and the works of man. They (the religious) boasted of themselves and spoke unkindly to others whom they told could never measure up. Well, guess what? We can't measure up, and neither could they. Jesus tore the veil. We are no longer under the veil. We are free in Christ, who saved us from sin. The veil is for sinners. When you find this amazing news, you will put aside your sin and die yourself. You will want to live for the King because He was gracious to save us from Satan's evil plan, which is to kill you and torture you forever. Satan wants to veil you so you can't see! If you don't believe me, that's fine. We get to choose. Nothing is forced! God wants the heart. What do you want? But please ask God to unveil you and see what happens. He will show up. Why? Because He loves you. Use Jesus's name. In the name of Jesus, there is power, a power in that name—Jesus.

In the meantime, I had a visit from the Lord early one morning. He seemed to come to me before my eyes, starting my day.

I was lying in the bed, and He threw a hand forward with His pointer finger and said, "I want you. I want you," and on the third time, He said, "I want you to believe in the supernatural."

As I was looking, there was a hand trimmed in a thin line, all around the outside of the hand, a red line outlining, and I knew immediately what the red line represented, and the words flowed like living water, covering my very being with pure comfort.

"You are covered in my blood. The roads you travel are covered. Anyone who believes in me is covered in my blood, covered in my blood. The roads you travel are covered in my blood."

I got up quickly and drew a picture of this so I wouldn't forget what it looked like. Whatever you are facing, plead with the blood. There is power, wonder, working power in the blood of Jesus.

"But, God, I already believe in the supernatural. I have seen you work one miracle after another."

"Go deeper. Believe bigger. Believe. Go out and heal the sick. Do greater work than I did."

"Oh my!" Now that takes faith!

Some may think the same thought of Romans 3:8: "If I do evil, good may come from it." Nope. It surely does not work like that. Yet doing evil may be pleasurable, believe it or not. We are even told that sin does bring pleasure for a moment. Yet it will bring consequences. Sin brings death. We will not get away with it. However, we all mess up, and this is why we need Jesus! Hello? Heaven forbid! If the heart is thinking this, it is time to rethink.

I know that Matthew 5:16 tells us to let our light shine before others. Why? So that they may see the Father working in us and give glory to the Father who is in heaven. He is the "I Am." If you follow Him, you don't have to walk in darkness. You may think, *I am not in darkness, and I don't believe this fantastic, made-up stuff.* Well, if you know what it is like to bump your big toe, you know it hurts, and the pain is intensifying. Life has a blanket over it called sin. We feel pain. Yet we all experience love at some time. That is grace.

When we die, life is intensifying a million times more, either on the darkest side or the grandest side. Either way, it is intensifying. You get to choose, and one day all the angels will get the command from the General of all Generals to go forth and bring it all to an end once and for all. It is written. When God looks at us who believe in Him, He sees His son, Jesus. Freedom! That is what frees us, His son, Jesus. ♥

It is such a relief to know that I can trust Jesus, that I personally become childlike in living and laugh like I have never laughed before, and it is good. We must present ourselves with the Son, who is our lawyer, when Satan comes to accuse us before the Father. We can never be perfect with ourselves and our works. If we try to present ourselves without Jesus, we fail. The scriptures clearly tell us that it is not by works that saved us but by the love of what Christ did for us to redeem us from the enemy who hates us and wants to deceive us now and eventually torture his prize. Oh, Satan knows how to work the system. Be careful and on the watch for everything that is not from the Father, but this is where the rubber meets the road and the line is drawn in the sand. I can love, and Christ can take care of the rest. Now that is peaceful. Amen!

We must handle the Word of God with truth. We are human. This is a hard task. This is why we need Jesus. He made the way, the truth. Now we can share the light that the Father of lights has to shine in others, to be the salt of the earth. He gives us the Spirit of self-control, which blocks out fear through His power that He has freely given. Amen! It is the Spirit of power to love as He loves us, and we do have self-control because He said so.

> If then you have been raised with Christ, seek the things that are above, where Christ is, seated at the right hand of God. Set your minds on things that are above, not on things that are on Earth. For you have died, and your life is hidden with Christ in God. When Christ who is your life appears, then you also will appear with him in glory. Put to death therefore what is earthly in you: sexual immorality, impurity, passion, evil desire, and covetousness, which is idolatry. (Colossians 3:1–25 ESV)

Some will say, "I don't want to give up the good life, drinking, etc. just plain fun for a stuffy life and attitude, and then I've got to go to church all the time! This does not sound fun to me."

My sentiments are you are not truly living until you have come to Jesus. He is life. He is love. He is the ultimate gift giver. Hello?

I am so filled with His energy and laughter that people ask, "Are you on drugs?"

I will quickly say, "Are you kidding? I have one brain, and what little I have, I do not want to destroy it with drugs."

"What is it? I want some of whatever you have. Your energy is electric!"

I tell them, "I am in love with Jesus, and you can have Him too." We just have a Jesus moment right there.

The apostle Paul said to be drunk in the Spirit. Do drunks care what others think? Nope. Do they offer up love and conversation with total strangers? Yep. They love people and are not afraid to have any conversation with you. Do drunks disagree? No. Usually, they are happy drunks, your best friends. Do drunks worry? No. Jesus is the wine, the best wine! Get drunk in the Spirit. Just love, and God will do the rest. Get excited about who you are in Christ.

If fear is present, are we worthless to the kingdom? No because Christ can cast out fear in His perfect love. What are you waiting for? When you have the fullness of Christ, you don't need drugs to free you. At least, I don't. I would be happy to share more if you are interested in what I would have to say. Just let me know if I can be of any help to you.

I was once lost and just lived without purpose. We can love because He first loved us. He showed us His love while we were of sin. He wanted to redeem us from the curse that fell on Adam. In fact, remember, Adam was the first to sin. Jesus is the "I Am," the second Adam not of sin. "It is finished!" (Beautiful . . . just beautiful!)

> I have said these things to you, that in me, you may have peace. In the world, you will have tribulation. But take heart. I have overcome the world. (John 16:33 ESV)

It is in *trust* we find in Him. I do. Hang on. See Him sitting next to you on the white bench, with His forearm resting on His right knee. His presence saturates the area with deep compassion that is accompanied by a strong desire to alleviate any suffering. The air around you is electric. You feel it swirling and see a rainbow of colors sparkling. You are in His precious moments with you right now. Feel Him. He is sharing with you the whole world, just you and Him, his brown hair flowing past His shoulders. He gazes at you. You are His masterpiece.

The strongest message is found in the blue hue of His eyes. They penetrate straight to your heart with an assurance of a positive declaration intended to give you all the confidence and support He had and has promised since the foundations of the earth, for you to be able to have the freedom from doubt and to carry out your work before you with the assurance of success. Yes, absolute freedom from timidity! He is the gift giver of self-confidence with the belief in your abilities because He gave them to you, and He is right there, all the way with you.

A smile of substance is found on his lips that speak softly without a word yet loud and clear. "I am here, your friend. Just you and me." His eyes and smile say it all. "Now go and conquer, for I am with you."

In Proverbs 27:17, we are told that iron sharpens iron, and one man sharpens another. We need one another. I want to thank all you Bible-believing, precious people for taking me in and sharing the best news of my life. I was so lost. The world told me I was dumb and worthless. I was not even wanted by the world, really. The world wanted me to believe the lies! But God was not letting go. He showed up in all of you. Thank you, precious family, for taking me in and sharing the gospel truth.

My own earthly family said, "Come home. You are in a cult!"

I quickly said, "No, this is the best thing that ever happened to me. And I want to tell the world."

Amen! We need one another in Christ.

CHAPTER 29

I Know You Are There, I Know You Care, I Know You Will Never Leave Me!

By trusting in the Lord with all my heart and leaning not on my own understanding, this certainly brings me such peace. Why? Because by doing so, I am trusting God and not myself. To me, that is a perfect place to be. Having assurance is a peace that passes my own understanding. Therefore, I absolutely know He is there. In my darkness, I would recite this: "I know you are there. I know you care. I know you will never leave me."

Things don't always appear correct. You can have total chaos, but this is good news to me. Why? Because I know victory is close and Satan doesn't want me to have it. So *rest*. Believe the Word and wait upon the Lord to make the way when there seems to be no way. Then He absolutely gets the glory because I know He did it, not me. Love belongs to the Father, and He freely gives it, even to the wicked. The wicked choose to love what they want to love. But God, He just loves. Imagine the world without love. One day He will take the beloved in a twinkling of an eye, and the world will be without *love*. Please don't be the one who is left behind.

> But false prophets also arose among the people, just as there will be false teachers among you, who will secretly bring in destructive heresies, even denying the Master who bought them, bringing upon themselves swift destruction. And many will follow their sensuality, and because of them, the way of truth will be blasphemed. And in their greed, they will exploit you with false words. Their condemnation from long ago is not idle, and their destruction is not asleep. For if God did not spare angels when they sinned but cast them into hell and committed

them to chains of gloomy darkness to be kept until the judgment, if he did not spare the ancient world but preserved Noah, a herald of righteousness, with seven others, when he brought a flood upon the world of the ungodly. (2 Peter 2:1–22 ESV)

But God sent His son to save the lost, and we know it is true that if a shepherd is out and one sheep leaves the herd, he will go out to find the one lost sheep, and he won't stop until he finds what is lost, and then comes rejoicing! (Matthew 18:13)

Please take a moment to listen to the live version of "Reckless Love" by Cory Asbury. There are many perfect examples of how people are being misled in the world to believe something they are not and lose hope. Somewhere in the darkness, God calls them out, and now look at what they are doing with their lives. It turns into fabulous testimonies, and others who get called out usually have a really awful situation, and they don't feel that they are loved or appreciated, lost, confused, broken. I am saying God uses bad situations to help others.

I see plenty of people with this feeling of hopelessness. I saw it just yesterday in the grocery store—very sad people, not one smiling face. Hello! Why are you alive? We should enjoy every moment. Finally, I saw a man, and I smiled, and he smiled back. After the many smiles I had given away, I found a smile.

"Wow, finally, a smile!"

He said, "What do you mean?"

"Many people are here, but not one can smile."

"Well, it's probably because they don't want to be in the grocery store."

"True, but I see sadness in the faces. We're here, so let's make the most of it! Be like Ellen. Hold nothing back." I thanked him for his smile, and he smiled back.

But in reality, people will turn to drugs or alcohol to try to break the feeling of unhappiness in their lives. I was unhappy, but I didn't turn to drugs because like I said, "I only had one brain!" I wasn't too bright. I could've been bright if I stayed with the Catholic Church because they make great, confident, smart people, but I chose to go to public schools for most of my life. I left because I had to fake taking drugs with my school friends and act really stupid and be the life of the party. They all love the high I got. No, I faked it. I had to get out of there. I returned to my last four years. (I couldn't take what was happening in the public schools!) By then, you know you're just kinda lost in the learning process if you never really learned anything seriously.

Even if you don't become famous or write great songs or become the greatest preacher ever or any of those kinds of things, God can still use you. You have a talent, and He wants to bring it forth, whatever that talent is. It could be being the best babysitter in the whole wide world. You could be the best cook in the whole wide world. Whatever you do, do it. If you are in love with what you're doing, don't do it out of murmuring and/or complaining. (I scrubbed other people's toilets!) Really? If we do complain, we will lose the lesson and be unhappy and misunderstood, like the Grinch. But me? I was Cindy Lou. Over and over, the vicious cycle repeats itself, and then we wonder why we can never find happiness when all along, it's right there, and we certainly don't want that now, do we?

I read in the Bible that if you can honestly say you love what you're doing and you have favor with man and God, that is an absolute true gift from the Lord Himself. Now I'm sure you want me to back that up with Scripture and where it's found. Of course, that's what the Scripture says to do. Back up your words with the Scripture because our words need to line up with the Word of the Lord, not what we think. It is found in Proverbs 3:4. The Word of the Lord is so precious and powerful.

> Behold, I stand at the door and knock. If anyone hears my
> voice and opens the door, I will come in to him and eat with
> him and he with me. (Revelation 3:20 ESV)

Please answer the door. He is knocking. You might say, "How is He knocking?" The world He created is His knock.

Ask yourself this one question. When you hear the strong mighty wind or feel a soft gentle breeze kiss your face, just seeing something that you know as the truth, ask yourself, *How did the truth come about?* Truth is a knocking so that you may know. It travels deep to the core of your being. It could be something as simple as your name, your dog, your home, your possessions, your mother, a child, anything that you know is the truth. These things belong to you. Who is the Creator of truth? Listen with the Spirit that freely gives to anyone who asks. I believe you will hear Him say, "I am! That I am! That I am!" Try it and really listen. Be very serious. ♥

Chapter 30

Truth Has Given Us All Things to Enjoy!

Abundant love knows no bounds. We all have been given a talent. We all have one. But you may ask yourself, *What is mine?* Be appreciative of all you have, whatever it is, for in your appreciation, that will open the windows of heaven as you give back thankfulness to the Creator of all of heaven and earth in any form. It could be your time, sharing yourself with others, money, listening to someone's hurts, sharing sound advice. The list can go on and on. Whatever we can give at the given time is our season of life. Give—period.

Our lives are a precious gift. We mustn't treat them recklessly. So many go through life feeling unloved. Don't. You are loved by the Great "I Am." Your life is treasured and so precious to the Creator. Don't play games with it. The light in your home (your heart, where your treasure is) is not trying to find perfection in yourself but sharing yourself. It is becoming the person God wants you to be and living out His plan through love. Love conquers all.

I was reminded of my precious daughter's words, "Momma, remember what you said. 'Love conquers all!'" as she found me crying and upset from the words of a person I knew hurt me deeply. She hit my heart like an arrow of strength to forgive them and move on. Wow! Thank you, precious Grace! You are not a mistake. You are loved.

> Now faith is the assurance of things hoped for, the conviction of things not seen. (Hebrews 11:1 ESV)

This is absolutely a word you can hang on to. All of His Word is certainly good to hang on to. But at times, in reading, certain words will jump from the pages for one's life and are meant especially for you at that moment. I believe that. But when you are waiting for the manifestation and you don't see it, believe it when it does come. It is a true gift from the Father, and you will know it, and He gets all the glory for it. Why? Because it meant a lot to you, and He just produced it through His promises, just as the scriptures said.

Now faith is the assurance of things hoped for, the conviction of things not seen. In other words, faith will produce the unseen that you have been believing. I will seriously raise my hands to thank Him for sure.

Chapter 31

Ma'am, Are You Okay?

One day I was helping my son Preston, who, by the way, has a huge heart, but his life has taken a turn for the worse. Certain people pushed him on that road God never wanted. I ask myself why another human would hurt another human. I can't wrap myself around this. We have a God who sees it all, and I promise you, all of you who hurt another human being just because you think you can, guess what? You will get your day, and it's not going to be a good day for you. God is bigger and greater than you perverts who use, abuse, and treat all with the wrong intent. Be careful how you treat children. They are the future. Think of these words. God is a just God, and He will make all things right.

Hmmm. Yet the Lord is able to use the roads we travel for His good to bring the very ones He loves back to Him. God turns it to good, and the Lord has called him to be a priest (and not in the Catholic Church either) to be a church for the people, for all those who hurt like he hurt, to live and tell his story. His story needs to be told. Why? To help others who can't find a way out of certain lifestyles or are being pushed by the wrong people, sending them down a road God never wanted for them either. In fact, these are the ministries we get called to when we accept Christ and ignore the very ones who are hurting us. You did find out that you have value and worth and that Jesus calls you a priest. You did know that, right? Jesus tore the veil. We all have the freedom to have access to the King of Kings and Lord of Lords! I am just saying. We call your mistreatment opportunity, and it is knocking. Hello? Gotta live it—for real!

Meanwhile, I was helping Preston with a flat on a very bad side of town. I was carrying on a conversation with him while he was working. My son was beaming with a new hope as I looked at him on his knees, working! I saw it. He didn't even know yet. It was like seeing a woman, and she was pregnant, and she didn't even know yet. But you do. You see her glowing.

As moms, we pray, praying continuously, forever. We need our children to see and know that they are loved and to overcome the evil plan of Satan. Preston's testimony followed from his lips of a positive change. I could feel it in my spirit, the energy of encouragement that was encircling us filled me to the point of overflowing. His heart was softened back toward the Lord. He never truly let go. But life had gotten so hard. Yet I felt a strong presence of the Lord moving in his life and those he loved around him in a positive way.

I suddenly was raising my hands in worship, in praise, looking toward the heavens, thanking Jesus. "Oh, hallelujah!" flowed from my lips. I was shaking my hands in worship. I was . . . really happy—I mean really, really happy—and the Lord was always there, walking us through. We mustn't give up. I was raising my hands as high as they would go and started praising Jesus right there in the parking lot, drunk in the Lord, and didn't care who saw me. I was not ashamed.

I noticed at that moment that a truck driver passed by, practically breaking his neck to look back at me. I mentioned it to my son. Oh my gosh!

"I know I am not that good-looking, especially in my rags, but a truck driver practically broke his neck looking at me as he passed!"

"Hmmm. That is strange."

Within a few moments, a police car drove up silently so as not to frighten a suspect.

The officer looked seriously into my eyes and asked, "Ma'am, are you okay?"

I realized what had just happened. The truck driver called them on my behalf. He thought I was at gunpoint. Oh my! I looked at the two officers and said, "Oh my goodness, Officers . . . I was praising Jesus for some good news!"

The two officers looked at each other and said, "That is a first," and drove off.

Thank you, truck driver, for making that call. I could have been in danger.

CHAPTER 32

Always Learning and Never Understanding

Always learning and never able to arrive at . . . the truth. (2 Timothy 3:7 ESV)

Now that is a sad state of affairs! In 2 Thessalonians 2:1–17, this is very serious information given to us. Are you really hearing the words printed to us, now concerning the coming of our Lord Jesus Christ? We should pay close attention to this, for Jesus is returning.

We have been gathered together to Him. How? Through the Word of God, the Holy Spirit. The things to come should not alarm us or take control of our minds with worries. In other words, we know the Word He has placed in the heart. How can I know this? Before I was saved, before I asked Him into my heart, before I told Him I was a sinner, before I knew that I could have a personal relationship with Him, He knew me. How? He whispered in a still small voice. He warned me of things to come. He saved me from the evil that tried to destroy me. That's how. The counterfeit comes claiming to be the god he is distrusting and is deceived by, trying to deceive you. "There is no honor among thieves," and that is what he is. That day will not come unless the rebellion comes first and the man of lawlessness is revealed, the son of destruction, who opposes and exalts himself against every so-called god or object of worship so that he takes his seat in the temple of God, proclaiming himself to be God.

Paul, in the scriptures, asked at that time. "Do you not remember that when I was still with you, I told you these things?" Paul questions them and reminds them. I believe this message, even though Paul said this thousands of years ago, is for us as well today. When I hear Paul, it's like he is talking directly to me. Amen! He is talking to us. This word that Paul is giving is for Christians already. We must know the Word. If you are not so sure of who you are in your walk with the Lord yet you desire to know Him, that is a great start. Just keep looking and know that He is madly in love with you. Talk with Him, and He will answer you. He will guide you. Just trust and believe and know He will send others in your path to help you along as well.

Philippians 4:13 tells us that you and I can do all things through Christ, who strengthens us. (Yay! Hallelujah!) The Word says in 2 Corinthians 11:14 that Satan can disguise himself as an angel of light. Be careful. He is an imitation. He "copies." He knows the Bible well, front and back. But again, have the mind of Christ, who conquers *all*. Jesus, the hope of glory is found in you. Do not fear Satan.

We need to cast all our anxieties on Jesus. Why? Because He cares. (This is such amazing news.) Pray, pray, and pray and thank Him for the answers, no matter how they may come, through man, a leaf, a rock, the sunset, a song—the list goes on and on. I like to look at it this way. He is the potter. We are the clay. We conform to the shape He designs. He pours in the liquid gold, sunshine, whatever He chooses, fills us to conform to the shape of the bowl, vase, etc., and we get to overflow because He never put a lid on us to stop the flow. We overflow like a mighty river with His mercy, grace, and abundance to share with others the very goodness of life. In other words, don't limit yourself because through Him, all things are possible to those who believe. You've got this because He's got you. For such a time as this, opportunity is knocking.

When things appear bad, I look at them as good. Don't get me wrong. It is generally a very painful time, and I really don't want to go through it. But I know that someone or something can learn from it. When I take it with that attitude and trust the Lord, I know He is more than able to turn it to good. I just have to trust, and many times, that takes a while, and other times, it can be answered soon. But I do know that the enemy does not want you to have it. I rest my case in Him. Faith apart from works is dead. We must have action in what we are doing, doing everything we know to do and then standing on His Word. Colossians 4:1–18 talks about us being masters. What are we masters of? We are all masters of our lives. What are you bringing in your life? Mumbling, contentment, love, hate, peace, worrying? What are you a master in? You are mastering your life, but are you getting it right? Now that is the million-dollar question!

The most important thing in life is how we treat another human being. We are all equal. In fact, one who places value on another is higher than oneself. Well, he is mature in knowing who he is and can live as Christ loved. I kinda wish the word *slave* was not used here. Why? Because a weak-minded person would think that he can own a slave. But really, what he is saying is we are all slaves. Slaves to what? Slaves to one another, placing a high value on one another. Why? Because that is exactly what Christ did. We are to be imitators of Jesus. He is the Master. Through this, the mystery of the Lord comes to life. Thank the Lord for everything and everyone who crosses your path. Some people are not worthy of loving. But when we love as Christ does, the picture comes to life, and the very one who is not worthy of love finally sees love, and that love brings them to their knees, and they know that God is alive and well. Oh, do you see the mystery of Christ coming alive? He lives in love and nothing else. By doing this, you and I are making the most of the time we have on this earth.

Oh, the ones who never understood this concept and mistreated others are suffering in torment, for they did not remember that we all have a Master, and He sits on the right side with His Father. He is the greatest planner to life. I am surrendering to the Master, and I will look at others with the eyes and heart that the Master has and still has for us all—*love*.

In Colossians 3:23, we see and hear that whatever we find to do, we do it as if we are doing it for the Lord, for His eyes see all things. I read this in the Bible, and it totally blew me away. If you think about this, I promise you will behave. Another way to look at this situation (He is watching you!) is that His name is not Santa, but He too has hair white as snow and wears a red robe. Hmmm. That does sound like someone we all know. We'd better get it right. Which list are we on? The naughty or nice list? Hmmm.

Colossians 2:1–20 tells us that our hearts need to be encouraged, being knit together in love. By doing that, we will reach all the riches of full assurance of understanding and the knowledge of God's mystery, which is found in Christ. All treasures are hidden and full of wisdom and knowledge. Paul said this so that no one may delude you with plausible arguments. He writes knowing that one day others would read his written message to us. "For though I am absent in body, I am with you in spirit." He is with us. I believe that. In other words, if you know what is found in the scriptures, you cannot be misled. The Spirit is there.

In Philippians 4:6, we are ordered to not be anxious about anything. I thought turning sweet sixteen was going to be the best ever. So I thought. Oh no, it turned out to be a broken heart, a lost time of reality, and falling deep into a world that I wish did not belong to me. I needed to appreciate every smile or conversation from the lips of those I loved. Life is so precious, and mine was tearing me apart. I went through the loss of my precious little sister, Rose. My life and my family went through a senseless loss. No one could comprehend the hurt. It hurt badly. I became a shell of a person, alive but so lost and so alone with respect of who are we and why we exist. I had a million questions as to why. I had taken things in life for granted, but I certainly did not think that I was. But when something so tragic happens, one can clearly and quickly realize how short and precious everything is. It's an unfortunate thing people do, and sometimes it is too late. People's lives, friends, parents, brothers, and sisters are priceless, really. We have to enjoy the moment, not the future, for that is taking things for granted. We think we will have a future, and we hope we do. Yes, we should plan for the future. It's the moments that count.

Being told that there was a God growing up, I definitely needed answers, and the Lord would have them, surely. So I started searching for the truth, the only place I knew to turn. Now with the Word, I can trust and give thanks in everything in prayer, making my requests known—but certainly not in a spoiled way but with a heart of gratitude in everything by prayer and supplication with thanksgiving, letting my requests be made known to God, such as protection for my loved ones and knowing God was able to meet the needs that we don't even know we have need of yet. Amen!

In Ephesians 4:1–32, Paul describes himself as a prisoner (yes, a prisoner!) to the Lord, and He urges us to walk in a manner that is worthy of the calling that He called you out of, whatever that may be—a drug addict, a thief, a con artist, whoever you were. That is your calling, to be delivered out of evil so that others can find the hope in glory as you now have. There are people in those same shoes and need you. You are needed. Now that in itself is great news. So many think they are so not worthy. You are. You are loved. Don't forget where you came from and how we are not perfect.

Using all humility and gentleness, add patience with love toward one another. Be eager to maintain wholeness of being united in the Spirit with the peace of Jesus. There is one body and one Spirit—just as you were called to the one hope that belongs to your call—one Lord, one faith, and one baptism. Amen.

> The natural person does not accept the things of the Spirit of God, for they are folly to him, and he is not able to understand them because they are spiritually discerned. (1 Corinthians 2:14 ESV)

Remember in Revelation 2:5, He mentions where one has fallen? He gently reminds us to repent and do the work that we did at first when you were saved. He is talking about those who knew Him and asked Him in and turned away for whatever reason. He said, "I will come and remove your lampstand. You will not be a light for others to see with. You and your precious friends, family, whoever we have contact with, will not have the encouragement that comes from our lamp." Be careful. We may cause others to stumble as well unless we repent.

The Lord wants a repented heart, a humble heart! In 1 Peter 5:8, we need to be watchful. The devil prowls around on us like a roaring lion, seeking someone to devour, and the Lord knows this and offers the Holy Ghost, who is the still small voice.

> [To] Paul, an apostle of Christ Jesus by the will of God, and Timothy, our brother, to the saints and faithful brothers in Christ at Colossae, grace to you and peace from God, our Father. We always thank God, the Father of our Lord Jesus Christ, when we pray for you since we heard of your faith in

Christ Jesus and of the love that you have for all the saints
because of the hope laid up for you in heaven. Of this, you have
heard before in the Word of the truth, the Gospel. (Colossians
1:1–29 ESV)

Finally, brothers, whatever is true, whatever is honorable,
whatever is just, whatever is pure, whatever is lovely, whatever
is commendable, if there is any excellence, if there is anything
worthy of praise, think about these things. (Philippians 4:8 ESV)

I really love this passage. Even when I can't see a way, the passage mentions
to think on good and lovely things, even when your world may be falling apart
all around you. I can gather strength in this Word. There is a peace that follows.

Now the Spirit expressly says that in later times, some will
depart from the faith by devoting themselves to deceitful spirits
and teachings of demons. (1 Timothy 4:1 ESV)

Ouch, ouch, ouch. If God is for us, the fruit of the Spirit will manifest itself in
love toward others, with a peace that passes understanding, joy that overflows in
laughter (which is a great medicine), kindness toward the human race, goodness
and the fullness of the love of Jesus, who gave all perfect gifts, and having the
patience in waiting upon the Lord's timing. Now who can be against us? Oh
my—great truth! Beautiful! The church of God is found in the people. We are
the church. It's not a building. Christ died for the people, not the building! The
Holy Spirit has made us overseers to protect the people of God. Christ gave His
life through His own blood. This word can be found in Acts 20:28

CHAPTER 33

Grace: Long Ago, the Lord Began His Work

I remember that day as if it were yesterday. I was a tall skinny seven-year-old, with long dirty-blonde hair, with my father's chocolate kisses for eyes. If I wanted to know what I would look like as a man, it would be my dad. He was a very handsome, gentle spirit, a soft-spoken man, and I adored him.

I got my mother's height and love for family. She had a quiet spirit about her with my father. She loved being a mother of eight children and one miscarriage. She was an educated woman and worked super hard to do her very best. I remember all the sacrifices she made for our happiness. As we grew older, we realized Mom needed a break, and we all chipped in and would take turns cooking supper and meeting her at the door after a long day at work with slippers in our hands.

"Supper will be ready after you freshen up!"

I have such fond memories. I absolutely loved being with her. She had taught us all so much. It is a fact that she always had us doing some kind of project, whether it was cooking, cleaning, ironing, mending clothes, yardwork, shoveling snow, painting, etc. Oh, the memories! Priceless! We love you, Mom! I also knew that there was something uniquely special about Daddy. But I could never put my finger on it. I would learn later just what that special thing was by the grace of God, and I'll share that later in the story.

Honestly, it's pretty cool how God works. He's such an amazing Father with a perfect plan. Even when I don't understand things, He does, and He works things out for the good of those who love and diligently seek Him. Even when we know Him not, His protection is there. We are not leaning on our own understanding, for we can't always understand His ways all the time, but we can know that His ways are higher and bigger than ours—Amen!—which leads us to the word *trust*, to know that He has our backs and is really something special for sure.

Back to what I previously was saying, hearing a voice . . . It was time for bed, and I was in my bathroom, finishing up my hair, when all of a sudden, I heard a voice call my name.

"Abigail!"

My thought at first was someone in the house calling me. I turned the hairdryer off to listen to see who was calling me. I waited a moment—and nothing. *Oh well*, I thought. I thought it must have been my imagination. I finished drying my hair, and I got ready to leave the bathroom. As I reached for the light switch, I heard the voice again calling my name. This time, I knew that it was not the voice of anyone who lived in my house. The voice was not one I knew. I froze. I could not move. I told myself, *Please go away, please go away*, squeezing my eyes shut, holding my breath (like that was going to help), and then to my surprise, it was gone. It left me. I just knew that it was gone, just as I had hoped. I was so happy I survived that encounter, and I never wanted to experience it again—so I thought.

I really was not sure what to think. But one thing was for sure: it was real, whatever it was. Scary! It was calling me again. I was afraid to tell anyone for fear that they would think I was losing my mind and lock me up in a nuthouse. (At this time in my life, I did not know any scriptures and was not encouraged to read my Bible. I had no idea that God had talked to people long before and that there are many stories of that happening.) Again, I knew that whatever it was respected my wishes and left when I had asked for it to go. The idea of hearing a voice so clearly was quite uncomfortable though. As quick as it had come, it was gone.

Chapter 34

A Simple Thank-You

Okay, yadda, yadda—not playing down what I am trying to say by the "yadda, yadda," but it fits. I think I have something to say, and I hope you are enjoying what I am saying, and I just keep going like the energy battery—yadda, yadda!

I really felt that I should put together my story to share with you that in my time of being unsure, the God of heaven showed up and assuredly told me I have worth, just as you have worth, no matter who you are. You could think I am weak-minded for saying this, but guess what? I have my moments, and if the truth be told, you do too. Absolutely none of us are perfect.

But I will say if you are perfectly well, okay then. I am not talking with you. I sound like a spoiled child right now. I can't change the heart. Only God can do that. I am simply saying you might think you are the greatest thing since the napkin! Okay, that's fine. I want to reach those who know that they are not and have been beaten down by the world or a bully etc. and think little of themselves because someone or something told them this. *Stop!* You are highly praised and highly loved by the Creator of the whole universe. You have value. You belong to the King of the whole universe. He loves you. You have something good within you that wants to be born and show itself to the world. You are walking in total love and don't know it. We are not a mistake, and He has a plan for you and me to live abundantly through the Son, Jesus, who provides wellness and all good and perfect gifts.

Even now, I question myself. But guess what? We do all we can do and then rest and let Him do the rest. Hopefully, someone, even if it is one person, hears. Then I will have a truly life-changing experience by bringing someone to the fullness of Christ—Oh, hallelujah!—by reading what I have to say. The answer to that is I will never know unless I try, and now I am sharing it with you. You may already have the self-confidence to believe in who you are. Yet even though I was loved, I knew that it was much bigger than my own thoughts of who I am. Your time is important, just as you are important. After all, you are taking the time to read this story, and I thank you for that. ♥ These are the stories I have wanted to share for a long time, and I know that God does not want me to keep this all to myself. So here I am, sharing, yadda, yadda.

Chapter 35

Mom, You Have to Write a Book

Paras rules with mercy. Well, he is the youngest of my five sons. He was learning to drive with me on the way to junior college. He would have to endure my storytelling of how great God is, how perfect He is, how He is an on-time God, even when we can't see it. He seemed to enjoy these stories but would often laugh and think I was making them up. Sharing these life lessons seemed like a perfect time to do that.

He later said, "Mom, you should write a book."

"Really?" I said. "I have been wanting to do this for a long time. In fact, your brother Sebastian—whose name has the meaning 'will, desire, a leader to save the people to Christ, to conquer and protect'—Amen!—was going to help me conquer this a few years back. But we obviously didn't get very far. Oops! We did not conquer. I will take the blame for dropping that ball. I admired him for trying to help me. ♥ I was going to do all the talking, and he was going to do the typing."

I wanted to share this with Paras, who delights and turns things into gold. He seemed to appreciate the stories and the realness of God and how He is always protecting us, even when we don't know we are in danger. Jesus has worked one miracle after miracle in our own lives and certainly will do the same for others. His gifts are for you too.

"Mom, you really should write a book!" He was persistent in this. In fact, he set everything up and said, "Now write!"

To appease him, I started, and to my surprise, I was loving it! I couldn't wait to get home and work on it some more. But then I thought, *Who do you think you are that someone would want to read your stories? Hmmm . . . At least I will have it written for my children.* Paras, you and everybody who has ever lived are writing books right now—everything you do and say, daily records. The pages are on a shelf in heaven. We all will give an account of the motives and why we do things. God looks at the heart.

In a vision, I clearly saw a flash of different blue lights. The lights were quite beautiful. Then suddenly, I saw steaming letters clearly flashing by in single file on a road zooming past me, traveling in time and space. I wondered what that was.

The Lord spoke and said, "These are the recorded words of every single person who has lived. They are being stored and saved and written in their books. Their very own book of remembrance. Good or bad, it's all there written. The bad things get blotted out when they ask forgiveness because they are covered in my Son's blood."

These words we speak may condemn ourselves, everything we have said. If we are void of Jesus's covering, we will know at that moment of truth with our own words as we see our lives flash before us. It is that plain and simple. You do not want to be without Christ. There is still time to make this serious confession of faith. While you are alive, there is time! He lives with an everlasting love. ♥ The Lord told Samuel that people look on the height and ability to believe from an outward appearance. But I simply look at the heart. What is in the heart? Why do we do the things we do? This is found in 1 Samuel 16:7.

Personally, I believe that is like the story of the Book of Remembrance that was told when Mordecai was due an award for saving the king's life. Esther's cousin, Mordecai, overheard a plot to assassinate the king. He met with the orphan whom he raised named Esther, who became the queen, and he begged her to go before the king and warn him that the order of killing all the Jews meant her as well. She thought, *I can't go to the king unless he calls me!* She realized that she had to do this even if she died doing it. The famous words rang out: "For such a time as this." She knew she was placed there for such a time. She was placed there by God.

The king allowed her to come forward, and she put on several feasts for the plotter, and the truth was revealed. The plotters were arrested and hanged. The king could not sleep and asked for his record keeper to bring the book of daily records and to read it to him. The story of Mordecai came up, which reminded the king about the two who had worked in the palace and who had plotted against King Artaxerxes.

The King asked, "How have we rewarded Mordecai for saving my life?"

"Nothing has been done for him."

Wow! God is perfect. Meanwhile, here came Haman, who was now plotting the murder of all the Jews, and Mordecai was first on the list. But little did Haman know that Queen Esther was a Jew. Oops! This plan backfired big-time.

> Then Esther, the queen, answered and said, "If I have found favor in thy sight, O king, and if it please the king, let my life be given me at my petition and my people at my request, for

we are sold, I and my people, to be destroyed, to be slain, and to perish. But if we had been sold for bondmen and bondwomen, I had held my peace, although the adversary could not have compensated for the king's damage." Then spake the king Ahasuerus and said unto Esther, the queen, "Who is he, and where is he, that durst presume in his heart to do so?" And Esther said, "An adversary and an enemy, even this wicked Haman." Then Haman was afraid before the king and the queen. And the king arose in his wrath from the banquet of wine and went into the palace garden, and Haman stood up to make request for his life to Esther, the queen, for he saw that there was evil determined against him by the king. So they hanged Haman on the gallows that he had prepared for Mordecai. Then was the king's wrath pacified. (Esther 7:3–7, 10 ASV)

Then those who feared the LORD spoke with one another. The LORD paid attention and heard them, and a book of remembrance was written before him of those who feared the LORD and esteemed his name. (Malachi 3:16 ASV)

Salvation has a race. Just because we ask the Lord to save us does not give us the right to live any way we want. It means we lose the old way and become new—"new beginnings." We will be known by the fruit of the Spirit of God. Yes, we have to continue to love and walk all the days of our lives in Him. Many believe that once saved, always saved, no matter how we act. "Oh, I will ask him to forgive me on my deathbed." Really? That is a selfish, wrong motive. *Wrong!*

Meanwhile, you missed your real life and His purpose for your life. The joy of the Lord is my strength in Him, I will boast. We must encourage one another to love. I find myself asking this very important question: What have I done to share this information? Really nothing, but it has certainly been in my heart to share for a long time. I know that He is working in my life just as He is in so many others, and I can't keep it a secret that would be wrong. I need to share these stories. My prayer is that the Lord has a big impact on you to know that He is surely alive and cares so deeply for us all. Not everyone will listen, of course. But it is all for His glory, and He is worth it.

Here's a flashback. My childhood home in Washington was really quite utterly delightful. The mountains and countryside were and still are strudel, with a forest of lush evergreens that spiked high so as to reach the heavens. It is simply breathtaking, the beauty of nature. I found in my heart that a greater force is at work. The five senses of life that we know rang deep within me. There has to be a God. The Spirit searches the depths of God, who is all around us, being open to see what eyes have not seen and having ears to hear what they have not heard. Hmmm. I've always enjoyed being in nature. I was quite an adventurer, hiking, climbing mountains, and swinging from vines. What fun!

CHAPTER 36

Last One In Is a Rotten Egg!

Years went by, and I heard nothing from my friendly voice. It was an early spring day. The weather was warming up, and we were excited that the swimming season was here. We would prepare the pool by putting some fresh water in. There was still a chill in the air. My brothers and sister hatched the idea and ran through the house, looking for Mom to see if she would allow us to play in the water while it filled up, and she said yes, to our surprise. The race was on. Who was going to be the first to get in the pool? The girls or the boys? The words flowed from our mouths. It was like we were in sync.

"Last one in the pool is a rotten egg!"

Mom allowed us to play as long as we could stand the cold water. It wasn't long though. Our bodies would be cold to the bone, and we would be shivering and covered with goosebumps within ten minutes. That was enough for us, but it was always so much fun. Looking back now, it was certainly a mind-over-body experience, to say the least. Children are so resilient, wouldn't you say? My precious sister, Aatikah, who is genuinely generous and has such noble qualities, was helping me with the straps on my swimsuit that seemed to be stuck and tangled up as I tried to get out of my wet swimsuit. Meanwhile, she noticed big red bumps all over my body.

She asked, "What are all these bumps?"

I assured her I had no idea what she was talking about. She seemed so concerned and worried that I remembered I asked her, "Am I going to die?"

Aatikah turned me around and looked me in the eye and said, "Absolutely not! Don't be silly. Mom, Mom, please come here! We are in the back bedroom!"

Mom came in, and I was asked to turn around. The bumps were mostly on my back and down my legs. Then I heard my mother say, "It was probably some kind of bug bites from playing outside, rolling around in the grass."

That seemed to make sense. After all, my mother was a nurse. My sister still looked very concerned and went to get some cream and began to blot it over the bites, as we called them since Mom looked at them and gave a diagnosis. But Aatikah, well, she knew in her heart that something was not right. I could see it in her eyes, and it frightened me.

I turned and looked at her again. "Am I going to die?"

She gasped and said again, looking me straight in the eye once more, "No!" with a stern voice. "You are not going to die!" She tried to look convincing and assuring, but I sensed concern, and she said, "You heard Mom. She thinks they are just bug bites," as she patted the cream on.

The next morning, I sheepishly walked down the hall, rubbing my eyes, trying to wake, and sat on the couch. I wrapped myself up in a blanket and sat quietly, watching my mother ironing. She started a conversation about what I would like for breakfast and looked at me and belched out a bloodcurdling scream. She grabbed me up in her arms, and we flew out the door to the car.

She was mumbling a prayer. "My Lord, please let her be all right. What is this? Her lip . . . her lips, Lord—they're huge! Please, God, help me get to the hospital safely."

We sped down the road, going at least eighty to the Air Force Base Hospital. Meanwhile, I didn't see my face that morning, and I really wasn't worried because my mom said the night before I was fine. I did feel a little strange in the mouth area though. My mother's prayer gave me a vivid picture, and it really felt like someone had placed a row of marbles in each lip.

CHAPTER 37

You Will Walk Again, But She
Will Never Walk Again

The doctor saw me straight away. I was placed on the examination table. As the doctor looked me over, he was asking all kinds of questions with my mother. Then he placed me on the floor to stand, and I collapsed. My lips were throbbing and were three times the size they should be. What was happening to me? I wondered. My rash had grown overnight into the size of small strawberries and now covered most of my body. They were everywhere. The doctor told my mother that I was going to have to be admitted.

I lost all movement and lay paralyzed for what seemed like forever. The doctor ran all kinds of test but could not find anything wrong with me. Day after day, my mother would come to the hospital and feed me. Eventually, I got use of my upper body and hands again, and I was given a wheelchair. About that time, the nurses had introduced me to another young girl who had been admitted to the hospital from a car wreck. The staff thought we could play in our wheelchair together. I had no idea what had happened to her physically at that time. I was just glad to have a friend to play with. She only had use of her arms like me. Day after day, we would have races up and down the hall. Oh, what fun! The nurses enjoyed watching us play (probably out of pity).

But one particular day I heard a still small voice quietly say to me, "You will walk again. But she will never walk."

I was happy yet deeply saddened by the news. I never shared with her what I had heard. But I knew that it was a true statement, and sure enough, I was walking again very soon, and I was able to return home. (I was unable to return to finish my third grade school year. The doctors were not sure if it was contagious.)

The day that I had left the hospital, I was heartbroken for that young lady. I knew she would never walk again, and I have often thought much of her through the years. But deep down, I knew that when I recovered from my paralysis, I had an audible word from God. I strongly began to realize that the voice was there to comfort me and help me along the way so I would have sincere compassion and the meaning of others in my life. Years went by, and I heard nothing from my friendly voice.

CHAPTER 38

The Fried Green Tomatoes

The South though is quite a different story in comparison to Washington State. Where do I start? No real mountains. The dirt was hard rock clay from the rich pitch-black soil that softly fell between my fingers from my childhood home. Boy, I remember my grandmother down in the Deep South of Alabama. She was in her late eighties, putting on her oversized ruffled lilac bonnet in ninety-plus degree weather with the humidity that comforts no one. It was so unbearable.

The farmer in her was born right in front of my city eyes. I knew that this was not her first rodeo. She gripped those two long bright-orange handles with black rubber tips at the end of the bars so tight, from the looks of it. Her body was shaking as she rattled her strong, steady hold, and boy, did she struggle to stay on course. Those orange blades rotated round and round, barely cracking the earth's surface. She held on for dear life, steadying so as not to move from the spot until it was pushing and scratching its way through the earth, at least twelve to eighteen inches. I had never seen a tiller in my life. I was completely shocked watching her, and I thought, I wondered, *Can she really grow anything in that soil, if that is what you would call it? Hard rock clay to me!*

By summertime, she had surprised me. She yielded the biggest, prize-winning, most delicious red tomatoes I had ever tasted and seen. I heard of fried green tomatoes and had to try them. I was hooked. They had to be a gift from God Himself, I thought, for all the hard work she had put into it. He just blessed her. That's the way things are done in the South!

My daddy was from the Deep South, good old Alabama. So if it was good enough for him, then it was good enough for me. Right? I wanted to go and see what all the fuss was all about. My mother came home from a visit down South one summer with my dad and my youngest sister, Rose, and Momma came home tryin' to cook fried okra. Now that was funny! Thinking back, it was not so funny at the time. It was definitely awkward.

Momma gathered all eight of her children around our oval green Formica marble table that everyone in the country had to make this fried okra. We were all so happy to be taking part in Southern tradition. Problem? Mom was tryin' to make it with canned okra. Every time she tried to grab a pod, it would slip right out of her hands and right off the table onto the floor! We all just stared at Mom and could not believe that people down South ate this slippery, slimy stuff. *Yuck!* we thought. We continued watching in horror as she really tried to get it right.

She mumbled, "You've got to be kidding me . . . What am I doing wrong?"

We thought, *Are we going to eat that stuff?* Over and over, we watched in horror.

Then she looked at us and said, "We will not be having fried okra tonight or any other night."

We were relieved. Now here I am, lovin' fried okra, fried green tomatoes, and pond-feed catfish. Yeah, that's what I'm talkin' 'bout! I got the recipe right. The unbearable humidity though, I can do without, hot and sweaty here in good old Alabama—but lovin', lovin', lovin' the people! "Y'all, cut on the light, ya hear?"

The climate was delightful in Washington, no real complaints. The temperatures were cool in the evenings. I remember the summer nights were so pleasant that my mother, brother, and sister would literally put an extra mattress under the apple tree and watch the stars far off and fall asleep. I recall August always being the scorcher in Washington. What do I know? The high was mid-eighties in the day, and by evening, it would drop to the low seventies. It was perfect and without the awful humidity that the South offered. I didn't realize how good I had it. Maybe I did. Thinking about it, it was not hot at all after living in Alabama. That was nothing. Roll Tide!

CHAPTER 39

A Great Warning: "Don't Turn That Corner!"

Years went by, and I had not had any encounters with the voice that visited when I was younger. At this point, I wasn't frightened anymore from hearing it. It seemed to help me know things before it would happen (my angel). Then suddenly—oh my gosh!

One day I was coming home from a friend's house. It had gotten a little darker than I liked, and I knew I had better get home now. As I was walking, I realized that a white van had gone by three times. On the third time, my eyes made contact with the driver. There was a cold evilness that ran down my spine, a sudden urgency of great fear. I could literally see deep into the presence of the sheer emptiness of the man's eyes that stared back through the windshield of his van—a heart of stone. It sent an alarm penetrating down to the very core of my being on that evening. My heart raced. I was closer to my home than I was to my friend's. So I started to run as fast as my legs could carry me home.

Then out of nowhere, a voice spoke and said, "Do not turn that corner!"

I stopped and tiptoed to the corner of the house and peeked through a bush and saw that same white van on the wrong side of the road, right where I would be if I turned the corner, and to top it off, there was no driver in the driver's seat. I had noticed as he passed me that last time that the van had those two doors that opened wide in the back.

My heart fell into my stomach, and I realized he was in the back, waiting for me to walk by and pull me into that van (but I was not walking). I turned back to my friend's house and ran like a cheetah. By the time I got back to my friend's house, I was out of breath, panting, and practically breaking down her door to let me in. I called my mother and told her I could not walk home and that she needed to pick me up, which she did.

Two days later, I was standing in my mother's living room, and the news was on. It was the same white van that had caught my attention and a photo of the same man whom I had seen who passed me three times the other day. The police had just arrested him for the murders and torture of young girls in the area. They had been looking for a serial killer who would capture, torture, and cut up the bodies of young girls. Then he would bag the parts and throw them around the town. He was one sick person.

Yet God had warned me. I wasn't even a born-again Christian yet. God had a plan for my life, just as he does yours, and it wasn't a sick man having his demented demons have their way with me. Oh, how I knew that I was spared a horrible death because of the warning that went out as the truth was unfolding that evening right before my eyes when the announcement was made of his capture! His landlord had gone to his apartment and found photos of the precious young lady who had been missing whom he had tortured and murdered.

CHAPTER 40

Our Home Was Filled with Sadness

The winds from the four corners of the earth shook the very foundations of our family life—a time that time cannot erase, such a horrible, very tragic day that the wounds of the heart cannot heal in this lifetime.

I was going to be sixteen in less than a month. It was early spring on the morning of that weekend. I had just walked in the door from spending the night with a long-time childhood friend, where neither one of us had any sleep. I walked through the doors and hung out around the house for a bit. I fixed a bowl of cereal and listened to my dad tell my mother he was going to the shop to have the snow chains taken off the wheels of the car. The snow had melted quite a bit, and I thought, *Yeah, those chains will tear the road up.*

My youngest sister, Rose, was looking for someone, anyone, to play cards with her. She sat down beside me, shuffling the cards. "Do you want to play a card game with me?" Those were her last words to me.

I politely said, "No, I don't feel well. I was up all night, and I haven't had any sleep. You know how those sleepovers work. No one sleeps. They should call them 'wakeovers.' LOL. But really, I feel sick. I've got to get some sleep."

She looked rather disappointed. I kinda felt bad for saying no. I heard her ask Dad, and he told her he was headed out the door to remove the snow chains. Mom was sitting on the couch, knitting.

I walked down the hall to my room that Rose and I shared. "I am going to get some sleep."

Oh, the memories of my early years with her! We would sing and tell jokes into the night until my parents would tell us to get to sleep. Our winters were brutally cold, and we would hug each other to stay warm as we could. Mom had even handmade our matching nightgowns with bonnets like you would see the girls wearing on *Little House on the Prairie.*

Finally, I was in my bedroom, ready to get some much-needed rest. The night before was fun and very long but certainly took a toll on my body. The bedroom door was closed, and my dog, Chocolate, was at the foot of the bed. It certainly wasn't long before I was sound asleep.

Then suddenly, I was awoken to the screams of my mother. It sounded so close. I sprung up, looking around, and in horror, I saw my mother frantically trying with all her might to help my precious little sister Rose. I was trying to understand what was unfolding before my eyes. I jumped from the bed. I don't recall what I did next. But the urgency was clear. *I have to help my mother! Oh god, no . . . Mom!*

My mother was frantic and trying to release her. I must have wrapped my arms around her young body. I had to pick her up to release the pressure so Mom could release her. My sister's body needed to be released from the pressure of her limp body. She was lifeless, just dangling. *What? How? Oh, my God, help her! Please let her be okay. She's lifeless! Her body . . . Please, God, help us!* We were both screaming and working and crying in disbelief and trying to think that it was a bad dream. *Yeah, that's it. I am having a really bad dream.* But this was very real. *Oh, God . . . Please, God, help her!*

This went on and on, a nightmare unfolding right before our eyes. We were frantically trying to release her, and finally, we got her carefully down. We laid her on the bed. We weren't thinking. My mother was a nurse. I ran down the hall to the phone that was far from my mother and dialed 0. I don't think 911 wasn't a thing yet. Zero would get emergency help.

At that time, you were asked to stay on the phone. I remember telling the lady, "I can't stay on the phone! I have to help my mother!"

She assured me I was helping by staying on the phone, which, at that time, I did not comprehend. "We need you on the phone," she kept saying, it seemed.

I did not understand this at all. I was so torn about where I needed to be.

She said, "Stay just in case we got the house number wrong."

I gave her the address again.

She said, "You must not leave the phone until help arrives!"

It seemed the dispatcher beg me to stay on the phone. All I could think about was my mother needing me to help her. I finally could not take it. I laid down the phone carefully, knowing this was the lifeline for help, and I rushed back to my sister to see if I could help my mother.

My mother was screaming, "Oh god, her lips are blue!" while she was doing CPR.

I fell to my knees and curled up in a fetal position. It did not look good. I got up and ran back to the phone, frantically asking, "Where are you? Please get here!"

When they arrived, I was relieved. They took one look at her and took me out of the room and closed the door. I will never forget the young man's face! We locked eyes, face-to-face as the door was being closed. I started to bang on the door.

I knew they were not going to do anything, and I opened it, screaming, "You've got to help her! Do something! You have to help her, please!"

He looked at me and closed the door again. The look on his face was "Too late. We can't help her." I fell sobbing at the door. My whole world turned upside down. It was like I had gone into a different time in space. Nothing was real. So tragic! I was in shock. I literally thought, *This is not real.* My life turned into slow motion for years after this.

It was such a tragic, emotional moment that day with the loss of my youngest sister, Rose, that I still get upset when I think of this day, let alone tell of that day. I can honestly say that some things never heal from the pain that runs deep of the senselessness of the loss of a loved one. I questioned God. *How? Why? She was here this morning, and now I will never hear her voice again. I will never share sweet moments with her again. Why? Why, God, why? She was such a precious little girl! My sister, God! The memories of her are all I have now! We had so much more to do and share . . . Why? Why? Why?*

For years, all I wanted to do at that point was to try to understand God. *Who is He, and how could He allow this to happen?* I searched and searched. I threw myself into school and sports. I really wanted to be left alone. I did have a few friends, but really, my goal was trying to understand God.

CHAPTER 41

Forced to Say Goodbye

Meanwhile, the pain was so great that I wanted to die. Your funeral was today, and I still thought this was a really bad dream. I just sat and stared at the people coming and going in and out of the house. I hadn't eaten in days. *This can't be real, not real.* People brought food over to the house, and I was so angry at them for even thinking we could think of eating. I wanted to throw it at them and tell them to leave now. *Food! How dare they bring food!* We were forced to say our last goodbye. *Life is not fair.*

I wanted to stay in the world that we knew just yesterday, before this happened, and not let go. Your voice will never be heard in this house again or anywhere on this earth. I will not ever be able to brush your long soft baby-blonde hair, to kiss your face and say I love you. No more songs to sing with you. Oh . . . Remember how we played in the tall blades of grass? Remember when Dad showed us how to go night crab hunting and how the water would wash away our footprints near the shoreline? I thought we would have so much more time to be together, to tell each other jokes, to climb trees and climb mountains, to play in the snow and make snow angels and see who can hold their place to be king of the mountain. But our story ended today. Who told the sun to shine today? How do I live today?

Mom and Dad are heartbroken. I don't know how we will get along without you. Why did you have to go so soon? I am sure this question will follow me the rest of my life. The pain is so great. I wish we had more time to celebrate life together. I really don't understand why.

CHAPTER 42

A Dim Light That Grows Brighter

I was at a great loss. I needed answers. I needed a purpose. Wondering why, I just crawled into my bed to try to escape the pure misery of the feeling of hopelessness. I wanted to die. *How can you be gone? How?* My room was dark, and I literally drenched my pillow with tears. The heartache and sadness was too much. I thought, *I am going to lose my mind.* I wanted to die. *How? How can my sweet, precious sister be gone from Earth? She was too young to die!* I was so lost. *I will never hear her sweet voice again.* Round and round, my mind went. I just could not understand how or why.

Then all of a sudden, I saw a dim light from the corner of my room. It grew brighter. I lay there, frozen. I could not move, even if I wanted to. It was such an intense situation. Every part of my being wanted out of that room, but I could not muster the strength. Fear had gripped me.

Then I heard a soft voice. It called my name. "Abigail. Abigail."

I told myself, *This is not happening. This is not happening!*

Then I heard these words. "This is not your moment in your life. And something beautiful is going to happen in your life."

Now I was thinking, *If I run to the light and turn it on, maybe it will go away.* Mustering all my strength, I rolled out of bed, thinking, *If I stay close to the ground, I'll be safe. But I still need to get to the light switch—and as quickly as possible.* I took a deep breath and went for it. I ran and flipped the switch, and the voice and light were gone. *What a relief.* But I stood there and thought long and hard. *Did that just happen?*

Wow! I told myself, *I can't say a word about any of this. The family might think I need to be locked up in a nuthouse. These kinds of things are not normal. Seeing a light, a voice calling my name. Yeah,* I thought, *it's best you don't say anything, Abigail.* But one thing was for sure. The voice did bring comfort. So I knew it must not be bad, and I thought about the words and realized that God had a purpose and a plan, and this was not it. The words gave me hope, and hope is what I held on to. *Really*, I thought, *how can I have anything beautiful in my life when life hurts so bad?*

I did not date in my high school years. I needed to find myself somehow. My little sister was a great loss. I just threw myself into my (all-girls) school and focused on my family, sports, and art, hoping someone could tell me about God.

However, I had hope, a secret hope now that I could cling to, and really, all I could do was cling. The words did bring me comfort. I had no hope, really. It's hard to explain loss. I still wanted the whole episode to go away as the voice was speaking to me. Can you imagine? You may be thinking, "Yeah, I am not sure I would be telling anyone this." Well, that is exactly how I felt for years, and I did not tell anyone.

CHAPTER 43

A Search for Truth

Meanwhile, I was in search of God and the reason for life. My mother had a huge Bible, and I began to read it. I remember a photo of Jesus in the Bible that I just stared at. His eyes in the picture had such compassion. I stared in hopes that He would come alive and talk to me. I liked the picture so much that I wondered, *Could I capture the compassion in my own painting?* So I did just that. Armed with all the oil paints I needed, I went to town. I painted a large canvas of Jesus, and yes, I did capture His compassion. I gave the painting to the nuns as a gift for my senior year. I could not understand any of it. I just read it in hopes of finding answers. I surrounded myself with people with the hope they could help me in my search for truth in the last four years of high school. I figured I would find God there, surely.

After the passing of my sister, she came in a dream.

I asked her, "Is there a God?"

She said yes but that He was mad at me.

I said, "I am sorry. Why is He mad?"

She said it wasn't her time to die.

Oh my! What did that mean? I then asked, "What is He like?"

She said, "I can't tell you. But . . . you will find out one day."

Then she walked down the road to a neighbor's house and told me something really terrible was going to happen here, and I woke up screaming.

A few days later, the teenage son who lived in that home was in a terrible car wreck and broke every bone in his body and had to wear a body cast. I really don't know why I had that encounter other than it proved to be true.

CHAPTER 44

Preaching Like I've Never Heard

One night it was late, and I wanted to watch some TV. I turned on a fellow, and he was preaching in a way I had never heard before. I sat in awe of his beautiful words and listened to him all the way to the end of the crusade. Billy Graham invited me to ask Jesus in my life and heart. I said the sinner's prayer. It was the beginning of something I did not understand, and it took years to manifest itself to me.

CHAPTER 45

Moving to the Deep South

My childhood was coming to an end, and I found myself packing up and moving to the South. The Lord knew what He was doing. I surely had no idea, yet I had been praying and seeking truth, and I found it in the South. Hallelujah! I would like to insert a bit of out-of-order thoughts here, but when I think about my move to the South, these are my first thoughts. Jesus finally called me to Him, and I got born again. He said in John 15:16, "You did not choose me, but I chose you and appointed you so that you might go and bear fruit, fruit that will last, and so that whatever you ask in my name, the Father will give you." Hello? Did you just hear that? Wow!

The Bible finally beamed with life for the first time in my adult life. I finally understood the stories, and I could not put my Bible down. Maybe I spoke too soon on being born again. That did not happen right away. It took years, and yes, I said I had asked Jesus in my heart while watching the Billy Graham crusade (the summer of my high school sophomore year). That was the start of my journey that I believe led me to the South. I really wasn't thinking about my spiritual life. But I believe that I needed a mentor, someone who would help me along the way. I didn't have that. I was like the parable where Jesus said there are four kinds of believers.

> "The sower went forth to sow his seed, and as he sowed, some fell by the wayside; and they were trodden under foot, and the birds of heaven devoured them. And others fell on the rock, and as soon as they grew, they withered away because they had no moisture. And others fell amidst the thorns, and the thorns grew with them and choked them. And others fell into the good ground and grew and brought forth fruit a hundredfold." As he

said these things, he cried, "He that hath ears to hear, let him hear!" (Luke 8:5–8 ASV)

I believe my seed was planted, and it was tucked away, looking for all the right ingredients to grow. *Look out, South, here I come! Now the fun begins!*

Meanwhile, when I had arrived, I was just living life, nothing unusual, but the seed I had received in my parents' living room was looking for the right conditions to grow. I wasn't a true Christian yet, and I had not heard the voice in a long time. I got married, and within four months, I was pregnant with my first child. Yay!

When my children were born, something magical happened. Holding and marveling over a child is one of the most fulfilling moments ever. *Holding my firstborn! Wow!* I asked God, *Is this that beautiful thing that is going to happen in my life that you had promised me when I was deeply sad?* It sure felt like it. But He did not respond. I got nothing. I thought, *This must not be it*, yet I knew this was quite a marvelous thing to behold. Children—oh, how sweet life is!

I had my second child, and God blessed me with a son, Wolfgang. It was during my third pregnancy when I had found out the real meaning of who I was, who others were, and what Jesus meant in my life, and I didn't want to live without Him ever again. I asked Him into my heart again and was baptized in November, one month before the birth of my second daughter, Hanna.

CHAPTER 46

My Adult Baptism

My heart wanted to be baptized, to go under, to come up new. I literally believed this to be true, and I wanted to be new. *That is His promise.*

> Wherefore if any man is in Christ, he is a new creature.
> The old things are passed away. Behold, they are become new.
> (2 Corinthians 5:17 ASV)

The strangest thing happened. I was raised in a traditional church and didn't hear the real truth or meaning about God, Jesus, and the Holy Ghost. I heard traditions, I saw rituals, I saw timings, and nothing was personal or, what one would say, out of order. It was clockwork. Even as a child, I knew when to stand, sit, kneel, and recite certain prayers, and most importantly, I did not have a personal relationship with Jesus. If they did teach this, well, then I was sleeping in "service." But I was told all my life that I was going to heaven because I was baptized as a baby. That is the one thing I remembered. Oh my! What a lie from Satan!

I never doubted who Jesus was. But a voice came and told me right before I was to be baptized. My heart, mind, spirit, and body understood the meaning and the seriousness of what I was about to do. All I knew was that I was told a lie all my life and that I wanted the fullness of what Christ was offering to me, and I wanted it more than anything. I wanted to do a total immersion under the water and come up new!

This definitely was a serious threat to Satan because at that moment, a real experience came. A dark supernatural side visited me at the lake (not the river). It was Satan's voice and was doing everything in its power to place doubt. The presence of the spirit of confusion was swirling around in my head (which was not from God). I thought, *What is this?* He continued saying that I would be making a terrible mistake. *Jesus is not who you think He is. He is a good guy, but He is not a savior. He is an imitator, and if you enter into a partnership with Him in this baptism, you will be making Him a God. And He isn't.*

He continued to tell me I was making an awful mistake. Wow! As soon as I heard all this, my thoughts were spinning. *Really?* I questioned myself, and in fleeting panic, I realized that Jesus had equipped me to rebuke it, recognize it, and tell it to leave now in the precious name above all names, Jesus. He gave me authority over the enemy. *And you will be gone from me now, Satan (in Jesus's name, of course)!*

> Behold, I have given you authority to tread upon serpents and scorpions and overall the power of the enemy, and nothing shall, in any ways, hurt you. (Luke 10:19 ASV)

Stop and listen to this beautiful song, "Down to the River to Pray," by Alison Karuss. Take a moment to reflex on the words of this song.

Realizing Satan was present, I immediately said, *Get behind me, Satan! I am going under, and I am coming up a new creature. You are a liar. You said some truth, but you twisted it. Yes, He is a God, and I will be in partnership with the Heavenly Father. Hear me now! Jesus is real. And I want Him.* I went under and, at that moment, covered a multitude of my sins and the forgiveness of those who had sinned against me.

> Submit yourselves therefore to God. Resist the devil, and he will flee from you. (James 4:7 KJV)

I wanted my old self to die once and for all. After reading my Bible, that was what the baptism promised. I wanted all the pain to be thrown into the sea, never to be reminded of again.

Here is a great song with all kinds of energy: "The River" by Jordan Feliz. Take a moment and seriously pause, reflex, and choose the river, if you haven't already.

> He will turn again. He will have compassion upon us. He will subdue our iniquities, and thou wilt cast all their sins into the depths of the sea. (Micah 7:19 KJV) (I am dancing on this verse.)

Now I saw that with God by my side, I was able to push through even when I wasn't a Christian. God's grace was there for me, even when I knew Him not "personally." Yet He knew me. I did not know. He knows the number of hairs on my head. He knitted me in a safe place in my mother's womb, and I was fearfully and wonderfully made. He would never leave me or forsake me. He held on to me, and He will do the same for you. It is called *grace*. I am not sure if you are aware that Christ's life was so full that if you tried to put everything in a book, it would be . . . Well, let's look and see what Scripture says about this.

> And there are also many other things which Jesus did . . .
> If they should be written, every one, I suppose that even the
> world itself could not contain the books that should be written.
> Amen. (John 21:25 KJV)

Chapter 47

We All Have a Story

This is a gentle reminder that even though I had struggles—but who doesn't? We all have stories to tell—my overall childhood, I thought, was wonderful. I loved my family and my childhood. Yes, there were a few serious situations in my childhood, but I knew my mother and father loved me. I felt loved and safe. However, yours could be a life of pain, a life of rejection, or it could have been a life like mine, loved but having struggles.

I pray that no matter what your life is up to this point, Jesus shows Himself, very real to you, in any manner that brings you to the fullness of His love. We don't have to look at the past to find what we are looking for. Sometimes struggles are there to help us look for a deeper meaning and cause for living. We don't have to look far. Jesus is there if you ask Him to be.

Or are you the one who has it all through your faith, only to begin to think you don't need God anymore? I know someone like that. This person even said, "I don't need God anymore. I have everything I need." This is a sad place to be. It's like taking a clear wall where you see the perfection of life and living the dream. You have everything, but you forget to thank the one who gave it to you. Oh, you think you did all this yourself! Did you? Oh, really?

You are smearing a pile of brown s&@/ (Forgive me!) all over your beautiful clear wall from top to bottom with your own hands, and now what do you see? Nothing. The once-clear wall is gone, blocked by your own dung. All Christ ever wanted was a thank-you. So see the big picture, please, the beauty that is surrounding us. So much of the unseen is seeing us through things, and He has a deep desire to have you as a personal friend. He, Jesus, is able to work with us and keep us. So have a happy heart, even in sadness. I had to hope, which He freely came and graciously gave me.

Later, when reading the scriptures, I learned that hope deferred makes the heart sick. Why? Because what you hope for doesn't materialize itself. God does not want the heart sick, and He gave me hope. He wants to give hope to you, which now means I can trust Him to bring it to me. I had my hope restored immediately in my Spirit, even though it wasn't overnight, and sometimes things come quickly, and others take time. But now I can rest in Him for the answers. He began to answer the questions I had, and through that, I was getting closer to a real living God. He allows us, you and me, visions of hope that follow my heart and your heart. After all, He put it there. I may sound weak to some, but I promise you, I am strong. Oh, praise Him! My Bible is so alive to me. I cannot get enough of it. The stories are as if I can see everything, like I was there. ♥

Remember I said earlier when I was searching for an answer, I could not understand anything that I had read in the Bible. Nothing made sense. I thought, *Gee, why can't I even get this book?* I just read it right away, even though it was over my head. I eventually found a verse that said the Bible is a mystery and God opens it up to those who ask Him into their hearts. Who knew? God did, that's who.

> Now the natural man receiveth not the things of the Spirit of God, for they are foolishness unto him, and he cannot know them because they are spiritually mysterious. (1 Corinthians 2:14 ASV)

When I was not really born again, I was in the natural state, so I couldn't understand things that were spiritual because I was not born of the spirit yet. Does that make sense? I hope so.

CHAPTER 48

Ask Him!

He also said, "My people are destroyed for lack of knowledge." He is basically saying, "You, who don't understand, are my people. Yet the lack of not knowing will destroy you." The information is there. But do you understand it? Here's an example. We know that water can drown us if we don't know how to swim. Knowing this, you do not get in the water to save yourself from the water. The same is true with electricity. We know that if we stick a key in the socket, we could die, so we don't.

But just because we choose not to hear the Word of God does not mean it can protect us. We must hear and know the Word, for it is real, just as currents run through a source of power to turn on the light. If you choose not to flip the switch, you will receive absolutely no power. Jesus is the power to free us from the unseen, which will one day manifest itself to us as true. We must ask Him for this information. He will give it freely to those who ask. James 1:5 tells me God is generous. He will not withhold from you. But we do need to ask. That is great news.

He said, "Freedom is found in me. I want to be with my Father, who is in heaven, but I leave you the Holy Spirit to guide you, teach you, and protect you." How cool is that? Being born of the Spirit of God reveals truth. We are all born out of water, from our mother's womb, which is of the earth. We must be born of the Spirit to understand the Spirit (water baptism?).

> Jesus answered and said unto him, "Verily, verily, I say unto thee. Except one be born anew, he cannot see the kingdom of God." Nicodemus saith unto him, "How can a man be born when he is old? Can he enter a second time into his mother's womb and be born?" Jesus answered, "Verily, verily, I say unto

thee. Except one be born of water and the Spirit, he cannot enter into the kingdom of God. That which is born of the flesh is flesh, and that which is born of the Spirit is spirit." (John 3:3–6 ASV)

Food for thought here. Some may say, well, the thief did not have to have a water baptism, and he got to go be with the Father in paradise. He didn't have to be baptized. Well, of course not. They aren't going to say, "Hold on, let's take you down so you can have a water baptism." Now that becomes an act. Jesus said so. That is all that matters. Jesus heard the man's heart, which was genuine and very sincere and very remorseful, and he was deserving of his punishment, and Jesus had done nothing. Wow! Beautiful.

At least four years had passed, and I had not given any thought to the voice that had visited me.

CHAPTER 49

Hidden in the Johnson Grass

It was an early evening, one hot July summer night. My first husband and my three very small children were headed to a small town to visit and spend the weekend with grandparents, which we did often. I knew it would be getting dark just thirty minutes into the drive. I never really liked traveling the country roads late in the evening, knowing it would be well into the night before getting there. But my husband did this sorta stuff all the time. He was used to it. Me? I was a city girl, and I never went from home, down country roads, especially at night. I still don't.

Everything seemed fine when all of a sudden, my husband was picking up speed on the two-lane road. I become very uncomfortable and asked for him to slow down, holding the children closer to me. At that time, children could sit in your lap if you wanted them to. Wow! Cringing right now. I think I need to thank God for His grace that we were safe.

Anyway, we were driving along at a high rate of speed. The more I asked him to slow down, the faster he drove, looking at me with a stare like he had surrendered himself over to a demon. I looked at him in horror, realizing he was not going to give me the safety that my family needed. I begged him to slow the vehicle down immediately. He got into a heated conversation, and he became noticeably angry. He was driving even more crazily.

"If you don't stop nagging, I am going to stop this car and tell you to get out," he said, to put it nicely.

Looking around, I knew that was not comforting to me at all. I was thinking we were in the middle of nowhere, and I surely did not like this at all. I sat thinking, *Speeding car, reckless driving, being dropped off, and possibly being exposed to the mercy of total strangers.* I did not want any of those options. The driving was so bad that I begged him to slow down. Nothing was working. That was when he slammed on the brakes and practically locked the engine up.

He was screaming, "Get the !&@ out of the truck!"

I took the children and stepped out of the truck (in shock). He burned rubber as he left us standing there. I immediately started looking around for a safe place to hide. I had no idea who was out on that country road that night, and I did not want to know either.

I walked over to the side of the road where the Johnson grass was so tall and thought, *Lord, the grass!* It was thick, and the wild weeds looked creepy to me. *There could be creatures and ticks, fire ants, lurking.* I was reminding myself to stay strong for my children. Suddenly, I had peace of mind to think we could hide in the grass. *It is at least three feet high. We could sit in the midst of it, and it will hide us. No one will see us on that dark road.* I was frightened, but I had a new faith in Jesus that He was assuring me to hide in the grass and that I would be safe.

Then suddenly, I thought, *What about snakes?*

Again, the still small voice brought comfort and said, "Hide," if I could find comfort in this situation. But He was there.

We did. All three of my children were sitting on one another's laps, and they were all on my lap. I'm not sure if that is possible, but it happened just that way. I wrapped my arms around them all in my lap and whispered a prayer they could hear, and we gathered strength from the words that Jesus was keeping us safe right now. *He knows we are here. He loves us. He will protect us.* Praying, trying to be strong for the children, I refused to cry and began to tell them of the Father's love and to never let go of Him and that some people will come into your life and try to hurt you. "If that happens, which it will, you surrender to the King in Heaven, for if one tries to take your life, you can rest that God will provide safety for you one way or the other." Not one child shed a tear for fear.

He drove all the way to his parents' home, and they asked him, "Where are your wife and children?"

He told them he had left us at a certain mile marker back on the side of the road. We sat wondering just what we were going to do, and we saw a beam of light shining on the road, looking in the grass. It was the sheriff's car. The sheriff had come and found us.

Needless to say, years later, I found out a few other things not worthy of writing down on paper of the kind of person he was, and we separated and later divorced. But several stories continued in our lives together, stories where the Lord was working with me and sharing Himself. You see, I was a Christian, and I thought that I could not leave my husband. *For better, for richer, till death do you part.* I just couldn't leave him. Boy, I had a lot to learn!

CHAPTER 50

A Serious Need . . . And He Looked at the Heart

Again, years went by—and nothing. President Reagan announced that a new law was passed about seatbelts and car seats for small children. Everyone, including children, had to be properly restrained. Well, we did not have enough money at the time to get a different car. At the time the law had been passed, we owned a truck, and we all sat in the front seat. I held the baby in my lap everywhere we went. Oh my goodness! At that time, that was how people traveled, holding babies in their laps. Yikes!

Anyhoo, I was concerned now because the law of the land was saying to properly restrain all passengers, and I knew the scriptures say to obey the laws of the land. I remember having a crying moment, telling God, *We must do what is right. So I am thanking you for the proper transportation to do so. I don't expect it to fall from the sky, but I do know you want us to do right. I just won't travel until then.*

Well, something came up. We had to go somewhere. I was so bothered by this. I remember asking God to protect us and keep us safe. I pleaded with Him and asked forgiveness and protection. We all loaded up in the truck and headed to our destination. We were quietly sitting in the truck, and I was holding the baby, and my eldest daughter had her brother in her lap. Oh my! As I write this, I think it is awful to think people did this kinda stuff. No wonder President Reagan made a law about this.

I was looking out the side window, and I heard the voice, and it said, "Pray before you get to the top of the hill."

I turned my head to look forward out the windshield and saw a hill in the distance. So I began to pray immediately. I prayed for angels to be stationed all over our truck—under it, on top of it, the sides of it, and anywhere else they were needed. I realized it was going to be a wreck, but I wasn't sure who or what was going to be in the wreck. But I told God, *You know where the wreck will be. I am asking you to place angels where they need to be.*

As soon as I prayed, a man as white as a ghost decided to turn his car right in front of ours on that two-way country lane, going about eighty miles an hour. I can still see his face as if it were yesterday—long jet-black hair and brown eyes, sunken, staring straight at me. Needless to say, we were safe. But my husband could not understand how we weren't all just killed.

I was shaking with excitement and said, "I was just told to pray for this situation."

There was such an adrenaline rush running through my body. I was totally thrilled that we were spared from a horrible, possible death. My husband just gave me a blank stare like "Wow! Really?" I often wondered, if I had not obeyed and prayed when I heard the voice telling me to pray, would we have all died that terrible evening on that two-lane county road? I think so. God was sharing His divine protection. Oh my goodness! It was like a fire was lit.

CHAPTER 51

Refusal to Pray

It wasn't that long after that incident when we were on our way to a family reunion at my grandmother's in a very small town in the South. By the way, God made a way for us to have a family van with seatbelts for everyone. Yay! He is so very good. The Father of all and perfect gifts, to be exact, says this:

> Be not deceived, my beloved brethren. Every good gift and every perfect gift is from above, coming down from the Father of lights, with whom there can be no variation, neither shadow that is cast by turning. Of his own will, He brought us forth by the word of truth, that we should be a kind of first fruits of his creatures. (James 1:16–18 ASV)

At the reunion, I was a fairly new Christian. Everyone was having a good time, enjoying the company of family. My son Wolfgang—meaning "path," "journey," and certainly "travel" (which he loves to do now as an adult)—was playing on a small riding toy when all of a sudden, I heard the voice.

It said, "Get your son, and pray for him out loud right now."

I thought, *I can't do that. All my cousins, aunts, and uncles are here. They will hear me.* I was so uncomfortable with the thought of me doing that that I flat-out refused and told God, *No!* No sooner when I had said no, his toy that was going straight all of a sudden took a strange turn and went full steam ahead, straight into a brick wall. My uncle Paul and I ran over to Wolfgang lying there on the ground, banged up and bleeding.

Paul looked me in the eye and commented, "I don't understand how the bike was going straight and took a strange turn like that. Did you see that?"

"Yes . . . Yes, I did."

I was so upset with myself that I did not obey what I had heard that I confessed right there to my uncle that I was told clearly to pray for my son and refused to pray for him. He looked at me like "What?" I also told him that I was afraid to pray out loud for fear of what they all might think. He had a very puzzled look and said absolutely nothing.

I realized at that moment that God was working with me to see if I would be obedient. It was a very sorrowful message to me because my son had suffered. He now had a head injury that stuck out at least three quarters of an inch. I began to think, really beating myself up. God was truly working, and I missed it and flat-out refused because of embarrassment. I had the car incident, but it was a silent prayer in the truck, and praying out loud in front of my relatives whom I hardly knew? I simply refused. Hmmm. Lesson learned, for sure.

Back home—not sure of the time frame of the last encounter with the voice, but it hadn't been long, as I recall—it was a beautiful afternoon to go out and get some fresh air with the children. Wolfgang saw a young boy playing on a toy four-wheeler, and he ran over to play and got on the back. They were just riding around in a huge field of soft grass. It seemed so harmless. It was a toy four-wheeler that didn't have a high rate of speed. I started chatting with the mother of the little boy when all of a sudden, Wolfgang was being flipped right off the back of the four-wheeler. I immediately called my church for a prayer chain on his behalf. ("Pray for such a time as this, and the prayer of the fervent availeth much." I knew these words were true, and I called on them in belief for my son.) I rushed to the ER. The doctor said that he had a broken collarbone. She shared the X-ray. The gap on his collarbone was at least an inch or more.

"Wolfgang's treatment for a broken collarbone usually requires a sling or figure-of-eight splint"—he was given the figure eight—"to keep the area immobile for several weeks. In some cases, surgery may be required. Most clavicle fractures heal within four to eight weeks. Physical therapy may help with rehabilitation. We will see him back then. Try not to worry and keep his play at bay" were the last words the doctor had said.

By the time we had finished up with the hospital, it was late. The moment we walked in the house, he was up running around, and I kid you not—he was doing somersaults. I didn't even know he knew how to do a somersault. I knew that he was completely healed. I called the prayer chain with great excitement, exclaiming that Jesus had heard our prayers.

"Wolfgang is healed!" I then said, "I am going to the doctor's office and ask for her to do another X-ray," and I did just that.

We were the very first one at the door of the doctor's office, and when the doctor came in, I begged her to do another X-ray.

She said, "Why?"

I proceeded to tell her, "God healed my son in the car even before we got home, I believe. I had called my church to lift him up in prayer. I got home with him, and he was doing somersaults!"

She looked at me as if I were crazy. I knew that she did not believe in the power of prayer or in instant healing. It was deep in her eyes. I was such a very young Christian myself. I had just recently asked the Lord in my heart.

She agreed and came back and said, "He will not need the brace. He is fine."

I smiled and said, "Thank you," shaking her hand wildly. "I knew it! God heard the prayer!" I exclaimed. I was a very happy momma.

CHAPTER 52

God Sees

Many years passed. The voice came in Hanna's own words and actions and took over in the Holy Spirit that one beautiful day. The Lord was teaching me about the power of words. A small member of the body can still make you steer greatly where you are going.

> Behold, the ships also, though they are so great and are driven by rough winds, are yet turned about by a very small rudder, whither the impulse of the steersman willeth. So the tongue also is a little member and boasteth great things. Behold, how much wood is kindled by how small a fire! (James 3:4–5 ASV)

I worked outside the home and had my children in day care. I did some on-and-off modeling and also had a regular job. I wondered why I even had children, only for someone else to raise them. It started to haunt me that I was working all day away from them, picking them up from day care, fixing dinner, putting them in bed, and starting all over again the next day. I wanted more time with my children. So I opened a day-care center. That way, an income would come in to pay the bills, and I'd be able to have my own children with me. Yay! It was a win-win.

It proved to be something I truly enjoyed. I loved every moment. It was not work. My day-care center was growing, and the idea of needing something bigger started stirring. The Lord provided a bigger home that had a double garage, which was a perfect spot for a separate day care center with a kitchen and everything needed away from my home. Of course, money was needed for things that needed to be done. A yard sale was the answer, and it proved to earn enough money for a fence at a discount price because one of the day-care parents had a fencing company. That was so great! God is so very good! Thank you, precious family, for reducing the price of the fence.

I still needed to have the garage door removed and a wall put up in its place, windows, electric plugs, exterior siding, and some other things to finish it up. I needed a loan at the bank. Being a baby Christian, I knew that God hated debt. But going to the bank seemed to be an option to get it done. Would I qualify for at least the loan just in case? It was approved. I could pick up the check the next day. I was uncomfortable with it, but I was happy. I made up my mind to go in the morning for the loan.

That very afternoon, the phone rang. It was a call from a man who was looking for a caregiver for his two children. He seemed like he had to find a place immediately for his children to have childcare the first day of the week.

He said, "My wife is en route with the children as we speak from another state. And I would like to come over and see the day care."

I said, "Sure. That would be great!"

It seemed that he was at the day care in no time. We started talking, and I asked him, "What do you do for a living?"

He said he was a carpenter. I was excited to hear this. Making conversation, I told him what I was wanting to do to finish the room. He seemed to like the idea and asked if he could help with the project.

I said, "Well, that would be great! However, I have a man whom I have talked to already, but he can't get to the job for weeks. What do you have in mind?"

He said, "My job doesn't start until Monday."

Remember, this was Friday afternoon, and his job started on Monday. I asked, "What are you saying? You can do the job before Monday?"

He said, "Yes, I can."

Wow! I could hardly believe my ears. I rehashed the thought. The local man whom I had talked to about doing the job couldn't start the job for weeks. I asked, "What would you charge me to do the work that is needed for the day care?"

As he started to talk, he pulled out a pad and pencil and began to write. He said, "If you are serious about me doing this, these are the things you will need for the work to be done." He handed me a list. "Can you get to Lowe's this evening and buy everything I will need?"

I said, "Yes, but how much will these supplies cost? Roughly?"

He said, "Around $500."

I said, "What will you charge me to do the work?"

He told me, and I thought, *Oh my goodness! I am not going to need that loan after all.*

He said, "I will be here before the sun shines. Here is my number. Call tonight to confirm you have gotten what I need."

At the end of the last pickup for day care, I went straight to Lowe's and bought all that was on his list, and he was right. It came to $500. Wow! He was at my home just like he said he would be. He went straight to work and didn't stop until he was finished. He did a beautiful job.

I paid him with a check and thanked him. I said, "Okay, great. I will see you on Monday with your children." I handed him the check.

He looked straight at me, and his eyes flashed like they were literally twinkling, and he smiled. *Twinkling eyes*, I thought, *literally*. I doubted what I had just seen, questioning, thinking, *What? I think I saw . . . Hmmm. Wow! Those are really special eyes*.

He said, "Thank you," and that was it.

He drove off in his run-down truck. I swelled. Feelings of rejoicing overcame me, and such an appreciation of the Lord's grace and greatness filled me to the point of overflowing. Again, I was so, so happy with this carpenter's work that I shouted from the heart with joy and thankfulness in knowing that God was filled with goodness. Even the birds take no thought, yet our Heavenly Father provides for them.

> Therefore, I say unto you, take no thought for your life, what ye shall eat, or what ye shall drink, nor yet for your body, what ye shall put on. Is not the life more than meat and the body than raiment? Behold the fowls of the air, for they sow not. Neither do they reap nor gather into barns, yet your heavenly Father feedeth them. Are ye not much better than they? Which of you by taking thought can add one cubit unto his stature? And why take ye thought for raiment? (Matthew 6:26–34)
>
> Therefore, I say unto you . . . Consider the lilies of the field, how they grow. They toil not. Neither do they spin. And yet I say unto you that even Solomon in all his glory was not arrayed like one of these. Wherefore, if God so clothe the grass of the field, which today is, and tomorrow is cast into the oven, shall he not much more clothe you, O ye of little faith? Therefore, take no thought, saying, "What shall we eat?" or "What shall we drink?" or "Wherewithal shall we be clothed?" (for after all these things do the Gentiles seek) for your heavenly Father knoweth that ye have need of all these things. But seek ye first the kingdom of God and his righteousness, and all these things shall be added unto you. Take therefore no thought for the morrow, for the morrow shall take thought for the things of itself. Sufficient unto the day is the evil thereof. (Matthew 6:25–34 KJV)

I said, "Oh my! I am so thankful for you and what you have done. This was an act of the glorious King, a good thing for sure. My heart is overjoyed right now!"

Monday came, and it was getting late. I thought he would've gotten here early. But then I thought, *Maybe his wife is going to bring them instead. He said he would be here early.* By noon, there was still no sign of him or her. I decided to call the number he had given me, and the recorded voice on the other end said, "No such number. Please try your call again."

I thought, *What? This can't be. I called him many times on this number.* Immediately, I thought of the twinkling eyes. *Oh my goodness . . . God, you sent me an angel, a real-life angel, to do the work.* I checked on the check that was written to pay him, and it was never cashed either.

> Be not forgetful to entertain strangers, for thereby some
> have entertained angels unawares. (Hebrews 13:2 KJV)

Wow! Wow! Wow!

CHAPTER 53

The Fire Ants Command Them to Go

My day care was up and running by the grace of the good Lord. After the fence went up, which was one of the very first things to be done, I did not realize I had a fire ant problem in the yard, mounds and mounds that had to be dealt with immediately. I remembered asking God, *What am I going to do?*

The voice said, "What do the scriptures say about that?"

I realized what I needed to do. I needed to take the authority given to me through the Son Jesus and command them to leave my yard.

> Little children, you are from God and have overcome them, for he who is in you is greater than he who is in the world. (1 John 4:4 ESV)
>
> And Jesus came and spake unto them, saying, "All power is given unto me in heaven and in earth." (Matthew 28:18 KJV)

His last words were "Father, forgive them. It is finished." Holy, holy, holy God Almighty! I was armed with the knowledge that Christ was bigger than the ants. It was a no-brainer. I simply used the power He has given to those who believe and told them to leave in a simple prayer.

It went something like this: "You fire ants, listen to the Word of the Lord. By the power given to me through the Son Jesus, I say you can't stay here. You have to leave immediately because I have little children who are precious in the Lord's sight, and He wants them safe. So go now. You have been given your eviction notice. The Word of the Lord says to stay out of the yard area, period. I know you were put on the earth for the purpose of keeping the soil loose for us, and I thank you for that. But I surely understand your threat and really detest you little creatures. So be gone. He told me I could ask this, and it will be done in the name of Jesus."

Just like, that they were gone. I never had a problem again. Seriously, you should try it. Hallelujah to The King!

CHAPTER 54

Take Your Words Back

I didn't realize just how attached I was to my little bundles of joy until one day a mother and I were talking, and this mother said, "If anything bad is going to happen, it always happens to Azreal!" She kinda laughed, not really meaning her words.

"Please," I said, "take that back. Please take it back." It was like she had taken a knife and stabbed me. I began to tell her, "Your words have power." I told her that Jesus was showing me this right now in my life. (Of course, I was a baby in Christ, and He was showing me things. I literally believed it to be true.)

She did not receive anything I had just told her. She left, and I began to talk with the Lord and said, *Jesus, how do I stop the power of her words over the child?*

He said softly, as He does, "You only have the power while the child is in your presence. You can pray for his safety and for him to have angels guard him while he is in your childcare. You can pray that the mother's heart will hear the words of truth you shared with her and for her to rebuke and uproot the words spoken. She is the parent. She has the power to change the words with her mouth, heart, and mind. It's not in your hands."

I prayed for him, this precious little toddler, so sweet and tender. I gave the situation to the Creator, and I rebuked any harm in my care. That was all the power I had, and of course, I prayed for the angels to keep him.

Then the day came when my daughter Hanna, who was led by the precious Spirit of God—oh, hallelujah—came to me in her frilly baby-blue dress, covered in petite roses.

"Mommy, Mommy!" she exclaimed with her thumb in her mouth (yep—thumb sucker, just like me! You go, girl!), being very persistent.

I stopped and bent down to her level. "Yes, what is it? I asked softly.

She said, "I would like to pray for Philadelphia [meaning "brotherly love"] and Azrael."

I was so surprised that I said, "How sweet! Sure. What would you like to pray for?"

She said, "For the angels to protect them and be with them. That is all."

That was it. We prayed, short and very simple, and she ran off to play. *How precious is that?* I thought. *Little ones . . . so precious!* My heart was warmed from her prayer—a wow moment, for sure.

The very next day, everything was good. The mother of the two young boys came to pick her children up from day care, and I released them to her custody. She left, and within a few moments, she returned to tell me she had forgotten a diaper bag.

I asked, "Where are your children?"

"In the car," she replied.

Everything seemed normal until the last minute. All of a sudden, I heard a noise, a crashing sound. I ran outside, and to my horror, I saw her car had broken through a wooden fence, plowing up toys as it was out of control, riding through the yard, headed straight for the other fence and over a cliff. I saw little Azrael was under the vehicle, being dragged, and the car went right over the cliff, with his little body underneath the back end of the car. The car continued down the cliff, mowing down the smaller trees. Finally, the car was lodged between several big trees and one giant tree in front of the car that stopped it in its tracks. I called 911 immediately. I did not see how anyone could have survived such an ordeal.

Before I knew it, the day care was surrounded with police, an ambulance, and the local news. The boys, by the grace of God, survived the whole horrible thing and were taken by ambulance. Azrael had a fracture in his precious little leg. But considering the situation, it certainly was a miracle that they were not killed. His brother, Philadelphia, was inside the car and was the one who had knocked the car out of park and into drive. He was absolutely fine bodily. But he was very frightened and crying something awful.

I immediately realized my daughter had prayed for such a time as this, for angels to guard these two precious little boys just a day before. Amen! I believe that prayer saved their lives. I wanted the world to know that God had sent his angels to save these precious boys and that my daughter had prayed just yesterday for them. But the news was not interested in printing the story of how God had saved them. I was so thankful that the two had survived the whole insidious incident. The prayer changed things, and I knew it!

CHAPTER 55

The Power of Words

Time passed, and I was very distraught, reliving this over and over in my mind. Every time I pulled into drive, I would relive the moment. I could not get it out of my head, realizing I was not going to be able to continue to do childcare. It was like this had happened to my very own. So I birthed a new business (with the Lord's help, of course). It was wall coverings and painting. I landed a job and was able to stop the day care.

While I was out of town, working on a big job, I came home for the weekend. It was a spring morning, and the windows in the house were open, just blowing out the winter dust. The fresh spring air was such a comfort. I saw the newspaper sitting on the ottoman. I noticed the headlines: "Child dies in a house fire." Oh my gosh! It was the same precious little child who had gone over the cliff, Azrael, the very same child about whom the mother said, "If anything bad is going to happen, it happens to Azrael." I was having a flashback of the whole thing again and thinking about what the Lord had said.

I let out a bloodcurdling scream and fell to my knees, wailing and rolling around the floor. "God, no! No, God, no! Please tell me no!" The whole neighborhood heard, I am sure of it. I rolled around, thrashing and wailing on my knees repeatedly, over and over. I wept uncontrollably, screaming, "Why? Why? Oh, God!" It was at that moment that I wholeheartedly understood the seriousness of the words spoken. Pure sadness . . . Satan was given permission through those words. My heart went out to the precious family. *God, give them strength!*

Chapter 56

Knowledge Is Given in the Nearness of Death

I needed a break. We needed a break. We decided to go and visit a long-lost friend in Florida. When we arrived, it was a clear, beautiful day. We decided we should spend some time at the beach. We had a great time playing all day in the warm sun, sharing the vast expanse of the open ocean, the breeze on our tan faces, and the sand squished between our toes. Need I say more? Even our two-pound chocolate toy poodle, Princess, seemed to be enjoying herself.

The day was at a close. The thought of leaving the beach was very disappointing and mournful. I thought, *How nice it would be to go out one last time in the water.* As I got in the water, I looked back and saw my Hanna, Trinity, and Wolfgang having a wonderful time, running and splashing. Princess was checking out the sandcastle, and Wolfgang wanted to protect the structure of his masterpiece, "The Sandcastle."

Oh my gosh! There is a song called "Oceans," and it is so close to my experience that I must sing it. God, the Holy Spirit, came through with knowledge on what to do at that exact moment once I confessed. "This is not God's plan for me to die like this!"

The water was up to my knees when I heard a woman who was under such pressure, her frail voice cracked from the strain of her body that had been fighting the raging waters trying to swallow her up.

"Please help me!"

My eyes locked on to hers, and I noticed another woman who appeared to be a friend was about to go under the water. She literally had no energy left. She couldn't even talk. Her eyes spoke a lack of . . . no, no strength left. I immediately realized they were in serious trouble.

As soon as I thought that, I thought, *Where did the ocean floor go?* I could no longer feel the floor. I turned myself around, and I was out to sea, about 250 yards. Oh my gosh! I could hardly see the children and the dog. I thought, *How did this happen?* The woman asked for help again. This time, I thought, *Lady, I can't help myself right now, let alone you. I panicked. I am in trouble . . . big trouble.*

Then I thought, *Wait!* Meanwhile, I was looking at my children and the dog. No one realized we were in trouble. Then I said, "I can't die out here like this! This is not the way the Lord wants me to go! My children need me!"

No sooner had I finished those words than the voice came and said, "You need to relax. Go with the flow. Turn your body diagonally. The waves will carry you back. *Do not* swim straight into the water back to the shore, or you will get carried farther out."

I actually did what the voice had said, and I was back on shore within five minutes. I was exhausted. Finally, my feet were able to touch the bottom of the ocean floor. I had to force strength into my legs with much effort. I was literally drained. I remember the difficulty to find strength. Heaviness gripped me. I was slowly dragging myself from the waters that tried to grip me in death.

As soon as I finally reached the people on the shore, I said, "There are people drowning in the ocean."

The next thing I knew, people were running to try and save the victims right in front of them drowning in the ocean. All I wanted to do was get my children and my dog and go home. I did not care if I ever saw an ocean again. I did not say a word that I was about to drown out there to my children. I just wanted to go. As I was leaving, I looked over to the side and saw the two women lying flat on the sand, alive but not moving a muscle. People were hovering over them. *Safe and sound*, I thought. *Thank you, God!* That was a very happy moment, for me to see them safe. I did not go over to say anything to them. I just wanted to go home.

Then I saw a man with his arms wrapped around the heads of two strong men. His limp body hung all the weight on the two rescuers. His feet literally dragged as he was coming out of the water and sand, and this was what he was saying: "I didn't need any help! I was not drowning!"

I said, "Just like a man!" shaking my head in disbelief, and didn't look back.

After that time, my marriage was unraveling for some reason. Moses said, "Give them what their hearts want."

> And there came unto him Pharisees, trying him and saying, "Is it lawful for a man to put away his wife for every cause?" And he answered and said, "Have ye not read that he who made them from the beginning made them male and female, For this cause shall a man leave his father and mother and shall cleave to his wife, and the two shall become one flesh?

So that they are no more two but one flesh. What therefore God hath joined together, let not man put asunder." They say unto him, "Why then did Moses command to give a bill of divorcement and to put her away?" He saith unto them, "Moses, for your hardness of heart, suffered you to put away your wives, but from the beginning, it hath not been so. And I say unto you, whosoever shall put away his wife, except for fornication, and shall marry another committeth adultery, and he that marrieth her when she is put away committeth adultery." The disciples say unto him, "If the case of the man is so with his wife, it is not expedient to marry." But he said unto them, "Not all men can receive this saying but they to whom it is given. For there are eunuchs (castrated) that were so born from their mother's womb, and there are eunuchs that were made eunuchs by men, and there are eunuchs that made themselves eunuchs for the kingdom of heaven's sake. He that is able to receive it, let him receive it." (Matthewa19:3–122ASV)

You guessed it—he was unfaithful way back, and I had forgiven him once. But he did it again. That was it. It was over. I wasn't perfect either though. But we both needed to move on.

Here's a flashback. I certainly was not perfect either. I ended up getting pregnant from another man. I was basically a single mom, already raising three children. *Oh my gosh! How am I going to do this? I wonder about what I am about to share. Should I share something so personal? Why not?* I started to pen it and erased it over and over. Again, I thought, *Should I? Why or why not? Someone, I am sure, can relate to it. It could shine a light in someone's darkest moment.*

CHAPTER 57

Realizing Sacredness

I became pregnant with my fourth child. I was a single, separated mother. My husband at the time said, "They will have to put me in a pine box before I divorce you."

We tried to work things out, and I had forgiven him for cheating on me not once but twice. Nope. Trust is so important in any relationship, especially marriage, and we were both guilty now! We were both wrong, and real love does not mean we can hurt each other like this. Being unfaithful hurts, and trust is broken.

Leaving was hard. I wanted to love him and trust him. But I really don't believe that was on his mind. At least, his actions did not show it. In fact, I became a real Christian because he started going to church before our third child. I saw a change in him. I remember thinking, *I want what he has.* Questions ran through my mind. *How could he be changed so radically?* He was changed. Jesus would forgive and cast your sins into the ocean, never to be reminded of again. *Really?* I wanted a new beginning. I desperately needed Christ. I was just as sick as he was with respect to the way we treated each other.

Read the following scripture. It says so much. It talks about traditions being broken once and for all. That is great news.

> For the law, having a shadow of good things to come and not the very image of the things, can never with those sacrifices which they offered year by year continually make the comers thereunto perfect. For then would they not have ceased to be offered? Because that the worshippers once purged should have had no more conscience of sins. But in those sacrifices, there is a remembrance again made of sins every year. For it

is not possible that the blood of bulls and of goats should take away sins. Wherefore when he cometh into the world, he saith, "Sacrifice and offering thou wouldest not, but a body hast thou prepared me. In burnt offerings and sacrifices for sin, thou hast had no pleasure." Then said I, "Lo, I come (in the volume of the book, it is written of me) to do thy will, O God." Above when he said, "Sacrifice and offering and burnt offerings and offering for sin thou wouldest not, neither hadst pleasure therein, which are offered by the law." Then said he, "Lo, I come to do thy will, O God." He taketh away the first, that he may establish the second. By which we will be sanctified through the offering of the body of Jesus Christ once for all. And every priest standeth daily, ministering and offering oftentimes the same sacrifices, which can never take away sins. But this man, after he had offered one sacrifice for sins for ever, sat down on the right hand of God. From henceforth expecting till his enemies be made his footstool. For by one offering, he hath perfected for ever them that are sanctified. Whereof the Holy Ghost also is a witness to us, for after that, he had said before, "This is the covenant that I will make with them after those days," saith the Lord, "I will put my laws into their hearts, and in their minds will I write them. And their sins and iniquities will I remember no more." Now where remission of these is, there is no more offering for sin. Having therefore, brethren, boldness to enter into the holiest by the blood of Jesus, By a new and living way, which he hath consecrated for us, through the veil, that is to say, his flesh. And having an high priest over the house of God. Let us draw near with a true heart in full assurance of faith, having our hearts sprinkled from an evil conscience and our bodies washed with pure water. Let us hold fast the profession of our faith without wavering (for he is faithful that promised). And let us consider one another to provoke unto love and to good works. Not forsaking the assembling of ourselves together, as the manner of some is, but exhorting one another and so much the more, as ye see the day approaching. For if we sin wilfully after that, we have received the knowledge of the truth. There remaineth no more sacrifice for sins but a certain fearful looking for of judgment and fiery indignation, which shall devour the adversaries. He that despised Moses's law died without mercy under two or three witnesses. Of how much sorer punishment, suppose ye, shall he be thought worthy, who hath trodden under foot the Son of God and hath counted the blood of the covenant, wherewith he was sanctified, an unholy thing, and hath done despite unto the Spirit of grace? For we know him that hath said, "Vengeance belongeth unto me. I will recompense," saith the Lord. And again, the Lord shall judge his people. It is a fearful thing to fall into the hands of the living God. But call to remembrance the former days, in which, after ye were illuminated, ye endured a great fight of afflictions, partly whilst ye were made a gazingstock both by reproaches and afflictions and partly whilst ye became companions of them that were so used. For ye had compassion of me in my bonds and took joyfully the spoiling of your goods, knowing in yourselves that ye have in heaven a better and an enduring substance. Cast not away therefore your confidence, which hath great recompence of reward. For ye have need of patience that, after ye have done the will of God, ye might receive the promise for yet a little while, and he that shall come will come and will not tarry. Now the just shall live by faith, but if any man draw back, my soul shall have no pleasure in him. But we are not of them who draw back unto perdition but of them that believe to the saving of the soul. (Hebrews 10:1–39 KJV)

He (my first husband) had told me when I first met him that he was not a believer in God, Jesus, none of that stuff. We were sitting, having a conversation, overlooking the beauty of nature in Washington. When I first met him, we were at a place called the Great Smokey Mountains. No, we weren't, but it sure sounds better than just sitting on the grass. But I was feeling love.

"Hmmm," I told him. "Wow! Look around you. How can you say that there is no Creator? Are you one of those who believe that it just evolved?" Now remember, I wasn't really a Christian myself either. But I said this: "When you and I see nature and all that is in it, I believe that there is a God who created it." (Later, I found the scriptures that backed my statement up—Psalms 19:1–5.) "Surely, you know that the heavens declare the glory of God. The vault of the sky shows us His handiwork. It is a treasure chest of known and unknown mystery. Jewels sparkling, the water bouncing off the glistening shadows of the reflection of all that is above. And day after day, He gives an utterance of speech to us through the creation. You can't deny it. It continues day in and day out well into the continued night. It shows us His knowledge. The moon offers us the light to objects below as well. He has covered it all. Yes . . . Do you hear the speech and the language of the voices found in them, the days and nights? Their line is gone out through all the earth and their words to the end of the world. In other words, creation is talking. You are a part of this marvelous creation of worship. Even the rocks are capable of worship. We live in a temporary shelter of worship, especially designed for us by the 'I Am.' Because one day we will move on to the place of eternity. Either good or bad, but I promise there is an eternity. But rest assured, we will be drawn toward it, for sure."

> Every knee will bow whether you believe it or not! It is that simple! And in all of the planning, He set a tabernacle for the sun, Which is as a bridegroom coming out of His chamber and rejoices as a strong man to run a race. (Psalms 19:1–5)

(Okay, that last bit was an odd statement, but if you really know Him, one can fall so in love that this statement is absolutely beautiful to one's ears.)

Wow . . . My husband is a changed man. Meanwhile, I couldn't believe that he was a changed man, and I had to go and see for myself how this had happened. I started going to the very church where he said he had found God. Wow! I was intrigued.

> Seeing that through the proving of you by this ministration, they glorify God for the obedience of your confession unto the gospel of Christ and for the liberality of your contribution unto them and unto all. (2 Corinthians 9:19 ASV)

I started going to the church, telling everyone that I was getting a divorce. I will never forget the look on all the church members' faces, like "Sure, okay, but you don't know the God we serve yet." They didn't condemn me for the words I was speaking and certainly did not receive them either, like water off a duck's back. But I also wanted to know how my husband was changed. I wanted what he had found too, and it was so. I found the answer.

We did not divorce. I was captivated by the love I felt in the walls of that church (which, by the way, were the people, not the building). I learned so many valuable life-changing lessons in 1986, and it all started as if time was in reverse, looking back only to recognize the wrongs and make them right—a new beginning, sorta speaking. The year 1986 made the number-one choice to know the true God: 1-9-8-6, 1 in choosing the number-one God; 9 being called to Him, a high calling; 8 as the wealth of knowledge; and 6 as the children, the family of God, being called for one choosing. Interesting! Add it altogether, and you get twenty-three: two is love, and three is communication. Two plus three is five, which is *grace*. There is nothing He has not thought out.

CHAPTER 58

Cleaning House from Generational Curses

I legally belong to the King. He is my Father. The one way I will learn what I have in Him is to get into the Word of God, and He does not want trash in my life. I must get rid of all the things I have allowed in not understanding what I had done by not knowing Him.

But He said, "Clean your house," meaning me and the physical home that I live in. Hmmm.

Curses can follow generations. He was making me aware, but there is beauty even in this statement. "How?" you might say. When Christ died on the cross, He took the curse and broke it, which means it cannot grab you when you realize the truth. This truth will set you free from generational curses. Jesus conquered, and we just need to understand, and then we rebuke it, repent, do whatever it takes so that the curse is not bound onto us. It is loose. That's the beauty of Christ's name, Him dying to free us so in our race, we are free from today's sin that tries to hold us. Every day we choose. But joy is found in this powerful news that we get so excited that we want to share this news to others who don't understand the truth. This seems overwhelming, but it isn't. Some things can be instant, and others can take time. Just know that we as Christians have victory in Jesus! Many good changes, good stories, are like water to the soul.

I was cleaning my house (spiritual), getting anything out that did not belong. One was some music albums. I had gone through them all, and the ones I was going to destroy were in a box. A "friend" came over to visit. I was out working on some new home decorations. She began to look through the box, in awe of its contents.

"Oh my gosh, I love this group!" she said, thumbing through them. "Oh, oh, this one too is awesome! What are you going to do with these?" she asked.

I said, "They are not for sale. I am getting rid of them."

As I continued to put together my shelf with the drill, she said, "What do you mean?"

I said, "They are trash."

"What? What are you talking about? These are great!" she said.

I took my drill and started to drill holes in them, over and over, and I said, "Now do you understand? They have no value."

She looked at me with a puzzled stare, literally like a stone statue, just looking at me, and then said, "You have lost your mind! You are crazy!"

I knew that she wanted nothing to do with me and my newfound faith. I was warned about this in the scriptures.

> If ye be reproached for the name of Christ, happy are ye, for the spirit of glory and of God resteth upon you. On their part, he is evil spoken of, but on your part, he is glorified. (1 Peter 4:14 KJV)
>
> Wrath is cruel, anger is overwhelming, but who can stand before jealousy? Better is open rebuke than hidden love. Faithful are the wounds of a friend. Profuse are the kisses of an enemy. (Proverbs 27:4–6 ESV)

I could not allow the fear of her not understanding my actions to control the situation. I knew she was not going to understand what I did. But I also knew that I was to destroy the work of Satan. What if? I believe it was a test to see if I would react with the fear of the Lord or the fear of my friend's understanding, and she did not. I never heard from her again. Did you know that Satan was in charge of music in heaven? I think he wins a lot of souls through music. He knows what he is doing.

> Thou hast been in Eden, the garden of God. Every precious stone was thy covering, the sardius, topaz, and the diamond, the beryl, the onyx, and the jasper, the sapphire, the emerald, and the carbuncle, and gold. The workmanship of thy tabrets and of thy pipes was prepared in thee in the day that thou wast created. (Ezekiel 28:13 KJV)

This is the Lord God telling Satan that he is doomed because he placed himself as equal ("I am a god").

> The word of the Lord came again unto me, saying, "Son of man, say unto the prince of Tyre (Satan)." Thus saith the Lord God, "Because thine heart is lifted up and thou hast said,

'I am a God. I sit in the seat of God in the midst of the seas,'
yet thou art a man and not God, though thou set thine heart as
the heart of God. Behold, thou art wiser than Daniel. There is
no secret that they can hide from thee. With thy wisdom and
with thine understanding, thou hast gotten thee riches and hast
gotten gold and silver into thy treasures. By thy great wisdom
and by thy traffick hast thou increased thy riches, and thine
heart is lifted up because of thy riches." Therefore, thus saith
the Lord God, "Because thou hast set thine heart as the heart
of God, behold. Therefore, I will bring strangers upon thee, the
terrible of the nations, and they shall draw their swords against
the beauty of thy wisdom, and they shall defile thy brightness.
They shall bring thee down to the pit, and thou shalt die the
deaths of them that are slain in the midst of the seas. Wilt thou
yet say before him that slayeth thee, 'I am God'? But thou
shalt be a man and no God, in the hand of him that slayeth
thee. Thou shalt die the deaths of the uncircumcised by the
hand of strangers, for I have spoken it," saith the Lord God.
Moreover, the word of the Lord came unto me, saying, "Son
of man, take up a lamentation upon the king of Tyre and say
unto him, 'Thus saith the Lord God. Thou sealest up the sum,
full of wisdom, and perfect in beauty. Thou hast been in Eden,
the garden of God. Every precious stone was thy covering, the
sardius, topaz, and the diamond, the beryl, the onyx, and the
jasper, the sapphire, the emerald, and the carbuncle, and gold.
The workmanship of thy tabrets and of thy pipes was prepared
in thee in the day that thou wast created. Thou art the anointed
cherub that covereth, and I have set thee so. Thou wast upon
the holy mountain of God. Thou hast walked up and down in
the midst of the stones of fire. Thou wast perfect in thy ways
from the day that thou wast created, till iniquity was found in
thee. By the multitude of thy merchandise, they have filled the
midst of thee with violence, and thou hast sinned. Therefore, I
will cast thee as profane out of the mountain of God, and I will
destroy thee, O covering cherub, from the midst of the stones of
fire. Thine heart was lifted up because of thy beauty. Thou hast
corrupted thy wisdom by reason of thy brightness: I will cast
thee to the ground. I will lay thee before kings, that they may
behold thee. Thou hast defiled thy sanctuaries by the multitude
of thine iniquities, by the iniquity of thy traffick. Therefore will
I bring forth a fire from the midst of thee. It shall devour thee,
and I will bring thee to ashes upon the earth in the sight of

all them that behold thee. All they that know thee among the people shall be astonished at thee. Thou shalt be a terror, and never shalt thou be any more."' Again, the word of the Lord came unto me, saying, "Son of man, set thy face against Zidon and prophesy against it and say, 'Thus saith the Lord God, "Behold, I am against thee, O Zidon, and I will be glorified in the midst of thee, and they shall know that I am the Lord, when I shall have executed judgments in her and shall be sanctified in her. For I will send into her pestilence and blood into her streets, and the wounded shall be judged in the midst of her by the sword upon her on every side, and they shall know that I am the Lord. And there shall be no more a pricking brier unto the house of Israel, nor any grieving thorn of all that are round about them that despised them and they shall know that I am the Lord God."'" Thus saith the Lord God, "When I shall have gathered the house of Israel from the people among whom they are scattered and shall be sanctified in them in the sight of the heathen, then shall they dwell in their land that I have given to my servant Jacob. And they shall dwell safely therein and shall build houses and plant vineyards. Yea, they shall dwell with confidence when I have executed judgments upon all those that despise them round about them, and they shall know that I am the Lord their God." (Ezekiel 28:1–26 KJV)

CHAPTER 59

The Bed of Lies

Satan is the father of lies. Our marriage was built on lies, on which it cannot stand. We were doomed from the first day we had met, and I don't say that lightly. Marriage is sacred, but my lack of knowledge hurt me, hurt us. But hold on. My children from the marriage were not a mistake. Without him, I wouldn't have had them. So in the chaos, God had a plan. But I needed to find it, just as we all have to find who is trying to find you, Jesus.

I was told at the end of my marriage by his best friend that he was an actual Satan worshipper. He even had a satanic bible. I did not know any of this. Had I known the scriptures, I would not have married him in the first place (but I didn't). Besides, I have three beautiful children by him, and they are not a mistake, for the Lord knew them before the foundations of the earth. There is a purpose in our screw-ups. It is called God's grace. I was not to be unequally yoked, yet I was. I was not a real Christian yet. I did believe that God was real, but I knew nothing and questioned not. I didn't know the scriptures.

> Be ye not unequally yoked together with unbelievers, for what fellowship hath righteousness with unrighteousness? And what communion hath light with darkness? (2 Corinthians 6:14 KJV)

CHAPTER 60

Conversations with God

Satan knows God is real. He knows the scriptures better than you and me, and he is in the presence of God, having conversations with the Lord, even after being thrown from heaven to Earth.

> Now there was a day when the sons of God came to present themselves before the Lord, and Satan came also among them. And the Lord said unto Satan, "Whence comest thou?" Then Satan answered the Lord and said, "From going to and fro in the earth and from walking up and down in it." And the Lord said unto Satan, "Hast thou considered my servant Job, that there is none like him in the earth, a perfect and an upright man, one that feareth God and escheweth evil?" Then Satan answered the Lord and said, "Doth Job fear God for naught? Hast not thou made a hedge about him and about his house and about all that he hath on every side? Thou hast blessed the work of his hands, and his substance is increased in the land. But put forth thine hand now, and touch all that he hath, and he will curse thee to thy face." And the Lord said unto Satan, "Behold, all that he hath is in thy power. Only upon himself put not forth thine hand." So Satan went forth from the presence of the Lord. (Job 1:6)

Meanwhile, my husband and I stayed together for another eleven years. I had a third child with him, my second daughter. Things were so great in the first year of us getting saved that people would walk up to me and say, "If I just had a tiny piece of the love I see in your marriage, I would be so happy." Seriously, that was a wow moment for me. But I knew they were right. It was heaven on earth.

But then suddenly, he was changed, just as quickly as he was confessing to know this Jesus that even I did not know. That brought me to know Jesus.

He was saying, "I don't want Him. I never really had Him."

What? He showed it with his actions. He was sleeping around on me again.

I had forgiven him of that once, but I said, "That is it! I have to raise the children. You could have AIDS! It can stay dormant for up to thirteen years!"

Our marriage was over for good as we knew it. We stayed together for three years just as a supportive team. Both of us were trying to find our way, but we had absolutely no procreation! I felt sorry for him, and I am sure he felt bad for me. We both struggled with what to do with our lives.

I asked, "Why did you do this to us?"

His response shocked me. He said, "I just did the whole church thing because I knew you wanted God, and you believed He created the earth and there is a heaven. So I figured this would be a good way to keep you. Even though I meant none of it."

It was like he had taken a giant knife and stabbed me right in my heart. I told him to please take it back. "You don't mean that!"

He said, "Oh yes, I do! If there is a hell, I will be in a cauldron, burning alongside your new boyfriend!"

"Please!" I begged him to take it back. "You don't mean that! Please don't say that!" It was a very sad realization.

CHAPTER 61

A Dream of a Stairway to Heaven

One night, while sleeping, I had a very real dream. My first husband and I were going up a flight of stairs that headed toward the heavens. We were so happy climbing the stairs. As I looked up, I wondered how much farther we had to go. The white fluffy clouds encased the top. So I really could not gauge the length. To tell you the truth, I really had not a care in the world on that stairway. God was so good to even let us participate in the climb. I was so in love with my husband. I was so happy, and so was he.

But suddenly, he looked at me with a smile and said, "You know what? I think I want to go back down a bit."

I just stared at him in disbelief. I noticed he was getting too far from me. I begged him to stop and come back. I pleaded with him. "Come back, please."

I was just standing there in shock, looking, and in the middle of the stairs, I was left by myself, watching him continue to go down. He went all the way down, and he was standing there, looking up at me, waving, and telling me to come.

"Come on down here. It is fun! Come. Come on," he begged.

By this time, the stairway had cracked in half, and there was a gaping hole. I looked at the stairway. I realized that there was a gulf of atmosphere between us, and the bottom half of the stairs were gone, an empty space that was colored in shades of dark blue, just like the galaxy had opened up and made a huge void of the once-solid stairway to heaven. The confidence I once had was proving to be false. The disparity, certainly, was creating a serious problem.

I started to cry, "I can't! I can't come down there!" and I woke up. I knew it was completely over for sure. No more. The end. We separated from each other—no divorce yet!

CHAPTER 62

The Evilness of the Voice of the Technician

Well, back to me ending up pregnant with a fourth child. *Really?* But you know what? God has a plan for that child, and the child is not a mistake.

> Even as he chose us in him before the foundation of the world, that we should be holy and blameless before him. In love, he predestined us for adoption as sons through Jesus Christ, according to the purpose of his will. (Ephesians 1:4–5)
>
> Before I formed you in the womb, I knew you, and before you were born, I consecrated you. I appointed you a prophet to the nations. (Jeremiah 1:5)

Remember, I am a Christian now, all the way Christian. I am a single mom raising three children and a fourth on the way, all because I slept with a man. Oh my goodness! I was in such despair. It wasn't the child's fault. I thought, *What am I going to do?* Morning sickness was always an issue with me. It would certainly make my life very hard.

My spouse came over and realized something was wrong and would not go until I told him. But I didn't want him to know my problems. I was so sick with morning sickness. He figured out that I was pregnant. He immediately offered to help me, and he would let the child take his name.

I told him, "Thank you, but I can't do that."

I can't believe what I thought next. Okay, don't be quick to judge others. You do not know what they are going through. I said to myself, *I will get an abortion.* He also offered to be there for me. Whatever decision was made, he would support me. We went to an abortion clinic. I could not believe that I had sunken to such darkness.

The technician called me back to the examination room. As soon as I entered the room, I immediately felt a gloom to it, like the whole ceiling and walls were covered in the biggest, blackest cloud ever. It hung over me. It was so real and eerie. She ordered me over to the table. She was cold and without feeling or emotion. She pressed the wand over my belly to see how far along I was.

She barked, "You are further along than you originally thought."

As she was poking around with the cold wand, I asked to see the baby.

She snapped at me in the ugliest way that was humanly possible and said, "Why are you going to kill it?"

I was taken back by that, but in the deepest part of my being, I knew that was God talking to me through her voice, which was so evil and cold, just as I felt for even being there. He woke me up. Satan wanted the baby dead. I knew I had to get out of there, so I did.

But what am I going to do? Three children and a baby on the way. Separated and wanting a divorce. Boy . . . what have I done? Well then, I thought I would adopt. So I went and talked with an abortion clinic. They were gentle and kind and offered so much hope for the child. But when it came down to it, I couldn't do that either.

I was headed home from work one day, and by this time, I knew I was having a boy. I remember talking to the baby by his name, Preston, and I started out with a message to my little one.

Dear precious baby,

Forgive me. We are going to get through this. It's not your fault. I don't know if you can hear all that is around you or feel the atmosphere vibrations outside your safe place. (I am lying to myself right now. I know you hear my and others' voices.) I am trying to make myself feel better in some way. What I am trying to say is . . . How do I say this? I took you to a place that kills babies. The clinic told me you were not really a baby! You were just a glob of flesh, nothing but tissue. I listened and believed them like I was in some hypnotic state. Their words carried the promise of death in your presence. I listened. You listened.

I took you to an abortion clinic and had discussions for aborting you. Oh my goodness! How horrible of me, your own mother! You heard the conversation. I am truly sorry. My life and the unknown future were the wrong motive. It was a very selfish act on my part. I am placing the value of your life as nothing over my own right now. I am saying God is not big enough to handle my problems, and you are not a problem. I am the problem. Yet God owns the whole universe and beyond.

I am feeling quite sick for having that conversation in your presence. Where is my shame? It was careless and unthoughtful. I was trying to sort out my own confused life. Please forgive me. You are the innocent bystander growing and forming into a priceless piece of art. You are special and a gift from God, and I was planning on destroying you. God has a plan and a purpose for your life. I need to step aside and let you grow in peace. You deserve so much more than I can give you right now.

My thoughts are I can't afford for you and provide a good life. I have too many unseen things in my life. The uncertainties, the unknown, can make one try to find justification as to why we do things we should never do. I am saying in my weakness that God is not big enough to handle this situation I am in. Oh, forgive me! I realize that there are good, loving couples looking to adopt a beautiful baby, which I am sure you will be. I need to find my happiness for your sake. I don't need to be a bundle of nerves and stressed out. That is not healthy for you.

Honestly, I am happy that I left the abortion clinic that dark day. The ugly voice helped me see the light, do the right thing, and try to sort it out, but I am still so confused. God never sends confusion! The road ahead that I have created is frightening. The uncertainties are what loom in the darkness. But I am reminded that where there is Jesus, light shines, even if it is a tiny ray. Hope can be found. I have nowhere else to go, and guess what? That is not a bad place to finally be with the Lord.

I will choose to trust Him in this. I know God's will is that you have life. I don't understand, with all this confusion I have. I could beat myself up over this. Or stop, just stop, and know that you are a child, a precious child. Oh, how I wish I could change the situation! But then if I could—which I can't—that would mean that I am making your life less meaningful again, and you would not be here right now. Do you see how messed up that thinking is?

Boy, I am forcing you to hear all these adult problems that I have created. Forgive me. But we are in this together, and I want to thank you for the heart-to-heart conversation. Thanks for listening too—not that you had a choice. You have helped me know and make the right decision. I feel your heartbeat, your little kicks.

I know now the least that I can give you is what you will need to grow—a shelter in my womb. Nine months. You are not a mistake. You were planned before the foundations of the earth, according to God, and I will let go, and let you grow. If I have to give you up when the time comes to a loving couple who are praying for a baby and holding on a prayer and a hope for a precious child to call their own, so be it. You are a beautiful gift from the Lord Himself—yes, you are—and I can't take your life just because the law says I can or because I think I can.

I must let go of myself. I can't change what is done. So I must find peace with the mind and be still in my heart and let God see us through. I really don't have a clue other than He is going to help the two beating hearts, yours and mine—that is if I will surrender fully to His will. The stupid, careless act that one finds themselves in—He is there to turn it to good. I must truly believe it. ♥

I cried out to God and said, "Jesus, your Word says, 'For it is God which worketh in you both to will and to do of his good pleasure. Do all things without murmurings and disputings' [Philippians 2:13–14 KJV]. *Let go*. I need you like the flowers need the rain, and so does this perfect, precious gift, my son, Preston. Please hear me, Father. I have really gotten myself in a pickle." I was just sobbing, driving, holding on to the steering wheel, having a conversation with the Lord.

No sooner had I said that than the still small voice came with a vision. I saw tiny hands flash up softly, and the word *piano* came.

The words were as follows: "He will play, and the whole world will listen."

Wow! Okay. I never offered a lesson but once to him, thinking that he was just going to sit down at the piano one day, and it would flow. To this day, I still believe in the word and vision, waiting. *Again, I have something to hold on to, a promise, as God cannot tell a lie.*

That by two immutable things, in which it was impossible for God to lie, we might have a strong consolation, who have fled for refuge to lay hold upon the hope set before us. Which hope we have as an anchor of the soul, both sure and steadfast, and which entereth into that within the veil. Whither the forerunner is for us entered, even Jesus, made an high priest forever after the order of Melchisedec. (Hebrews 6:18–20 KJV)

Where there is no vision, the people perish, but he that keepeth the law, happy is he. (Proverbs 29:18 KJV)

Oh my goodness! His Word to us is so alive. Hallelujah to the King of Kings! In all this, I have learned that we cannot change a person. But we can pray for them. People are going to hurt us, and we are going to hurt people. Most people don't intentionally want to hurt you. But it happens. This is why we need a savior. We are not perfect.

Now where am I in the story? Hmmm . . . God provided a new husband, and he was a Christian. I was thrilled. I figured if we have God, we have everything. Within a year, baby Sebastian arrived—eleven pounds, fifteen ounces, completely natural birth. Sebastian stands for "my people," "the protector." The day of his birth was, of course, a joyous time.

During the contractions, I danced with the nurse. I remember her asking, "Oh my! You are having a big contraction. Do you feel it?" *Pain? Really? This is a joyous time!* Being saved was a whole different experience from giving birth. I actually enjoyed the whole process. The pushing part was the best feeling ever. Ha . . .

Here's a flashback. Things were a whole different ball game when I had my first child, Trinity. My mother talked me into natural childbirth. She taught Lamaze classes, and I went to all of them. The one thing I remembered was the breathing and staying focused on one thing in the room. I bought a giant lollipop to look at, with all the beautiful colors of the swirls (Do you remember those?) in hopes of getting carried away in a trance, spinning and spinning. It didn't happen. It was a nice thought though.

My mother was a nurse, and I trusted her. After all, she was my mother, right? She knew best, right? Anyhoo, that turned out to be the biggest mistake of my life. Not really. At least, at the moment, I thought so. No, fear was her advice—really. Ha! Can you say fear gripped me big time? A thousand times? That was my experience. Awful. The birth canal, the bones opening up for the first time. Crazy! I do not recommend a natural birth for a first-time mom. No, no! Your bones are opening up for the very first time. Not fun, but you too will get through it.

I almost killed the nurse who had gotten too close to me. I was delusional, to say the least. I said, "Lady . . . *you* are going to feel this pain with me, my pain, and I am going to share it with you. There is plenty! My momma always told me to share. Right, Mother?"

I squeezed her so hard, she could hardly breathe. I literally thought she was turning blue. One nurse ran out to get others to come in and pry her from my death grip. Next thing I knew, the room was filled with doctors and nurses doing everything they could to help this poor nurse release my grip on her. I think she got to go home. Ha!

I remembered saying, "I am going to have a serious word with Eve and tell Adam thanks for listening to Eve! You have cursed all the generations giving birth! Thanks! Thanks a lot!"

Unto the woman, he said, "I will greatly multiply thy

sorrow and thy conception. In sorrow, thou shalt bring forth children, and thy desire shall be to thy husband, and he shall rule over thee." And unto Adam, he said, "Because thou hast hearkened unto the voice of thy wife and hast eaten of the tree, of which I commanded thee, saying, 'Thou shalt not eat of it,' cursed is the ground for thy sake. In sorrow shalt thou eat of it all the days of thy life." (Genesis 3:16–17 KJV)

I begged the doctor to cut me open and get this baby out. I was literally screaming. I even cussed in the presence of my mother. "#€*> this!" Now that is something I would never do. In fact, I don't think I even knew that word. I certainly don't recall saying it. My mother told me all this bad behavior I did.

"Mother! I did not! I did not say and do that! Did I?" I was so shocked. She wouldn't tell that lie.

I do recall imagining that I had a black cast-iron pan and I was hitting everyone in the delivery room with it. That must have been the time I threw in those absurdities. Me and my big mouth!

Before entering the delivery room, I spoke and said to the doctor, "I know a lot of women are having C-sections these days because they want to. But I don't want that at all. I plan on having this baby the way God intended me to have this baby. I need you to know this, Doctor." They were wheeling me to the delivery room at that time. "*Do not* cut me open."

The doctor looked at my mother, who was with me, and said, "Did you just hear that?"

Then I screamed, "Get this baby out now! Cut me open! Get it out!"

The doctor said the following words: "Oh no! Remember, you are going to have this baby the way God intended."

I had to brave up and stay focused. *Great.* What else was I going to do? Nothing. I was stuck. Me and my lollipop! All I could think about was how mad I was at Adam and Eve for bringing this curse. I did know a little about my Bible at that time in my life. Hmmm.

The moment I held her in my arms, my heart melted, and I said, "I am ready to do this again."

"Again?" said the doctor, who was a very good friend of my mother. He astonishingly looked at my mother in disbelief and said, "Did you just hear that?"

As I lay there, I whispered, "God, is this that beautiful thing you told me about years ago?"

Whenever a woman is in labor, she has pain because her hour has come, but when she gives birth to the child, she no

longer remembers the anguish because of the joy that a child
has been born into the world. (John 16:21)

Back to Sebastian's story . . . When the moment of truth came, it got real quiet
in the room. The baby was being pushed out. I was fine. But you could hear a pin
drop. I thought, *Well, this is strange, staying focused and concentrating on having a child.
Breathe, pant, hold, wait, and push!* Anyone out there relate?

When Sebastian arrived, I was thrilled like most mommas—not like that. His
head was bruised like he had worn a motorcycle helmet. He was huge! He looked
three months old to me at least, just big—and long too. He had a hint of red hair
that turned snow white as he grew, and his eyes—oh, the blue!

The head nurse came in and said when the doctor realized how big the baby
was, he had a heart attack. Sebastian had an intestinal and stomach issue that
made him projectile his breast milk. He became a very sick little boy. It took
weeks to figure out what was happening. They said he had holes in the walls of his
intestines, and surgery would be needed to remove a lot of the damaged intestines.
I listened, and I would not deny my son's help. But I also knew that prayer changes
things, and God did not want my son to suffer. He could heal him. I began to
search my heart and realized that my husband and I had sinned. I had a flash
of truth enter my being and knew we had to get forgiveness from the Father, and
these scriptures confirmed it.

Keeping steadfast love for thousands, forgiving the iniquity and
transgression and sin, but I who will by no means clear the guilty ones,
visiting the iniquity of the fathers on the children and the children's
children, to the third and the fourth generation. (Exodus 34:7)

Sin can follow you for generations. But our sin was closer to home, our
own lives.

The LORD is slow to anger and abounding in steadfast
love, forgiving iniquity, and transgression, but he will by no
means clear the guilty, visiting the iniquity of the fathers on
the children, to the third and the fourth generation. (Numbers
14:18)

I went to my husband and said, "We have sinned, and we must ask God to
forgive us. Our son needs us."

We got down on our knees, and we both cried out to our King.

He said, "You can come to the throne and humble yourself and ask
forgiveness."

We cried our hearts out to the Lord there on our bathroom floor. I also had a prayer partner whom the Lord directed me to, my sister-in-law. She had a godly heart, and we began to lift this precious baby up.

Within days, the doctor said, "The X-ray is showing that his intestines are healing on their own."

I was elated with joy. God heard our prayers. I did not mention our prayers to the doctor. It was so personal to us, and at the time, I just did not go there.

The doctor did say, "Years ago, when a baby was born with this condition, they just died. This is normally found in premature babies. And we know by the size of him that he was not premature." Actually, he had one whole month before he was to be born.

I went to the doctor. "I can't go another day! I can't breathe!"

He ordered an ultrasound. "His size is at least nine pounds. The only thing I would be concerned with would be his lungs."

"I cannot breathe! Please!"

The doctor finally agreed. Time went by, and he was growing fast and round. The child was so big. It was such a joyous time. He was such a beautiful baby boy. I did not encourage him to walk. He literally rolled around the room. Even when it was time to walk, he didn't, and I didn't encourage it either. I was concerned his bones could not support the weight and cause bow legs.

Now he is six feet and five inches, a thin young man doing amazing things with his young life. I am so proud of him and his accomplishments! He has a deep love for the Lord, and he is a seeker of truth. Again, Jesus is awesome, Within a year of my marriage, I had all my children living with me and another baby boy.

It wasn't long before my ex stuck his ugly head up and worked a number on my first three children—offering the moon, if he could, to him. He was doing everything in his power to convince them to live with him. My son longed for a relationship with his father, and really, what son wouldn't want that? He was promising him the moon.

My son Wolfgang asked, "Mom, if I stay here with you, what will you buy me? A four-wheeler?"

I said, "Nope. I am not going to buy your love. I will, however, give you my love and hopefully a happy home where you grow strong in who you are as a young man."

Well, his dad bought him a motorcycle that the two of them would work on, which never happened. He moved out along with the youngest daughter at the time, Hanna. The court said it was best to keep the children together. Life was a nightmare, being without my children. I had never dreamed that I would be without two of my first three children.

CHAPTER 63

The Lord Calls Me in the Night

I learned this fact in Isaiah 50:4. I could not sleep. Did you know that if you cannot sleep, it is the Lord wanting to have conversation and time with you? God is giving you answers to your problems and for a word to give to someone else who is looking for answers. He is into details. Hallelujah!

> Arise, cry out in the night. In the beginning of the watches, pour out thine heart like water before the face of the Lord, lift up thy hands toward him for the life of thy young children that faint for hunger in the top of every street. (Lamentations 2:19 KJV)
>
> The Lord God hath given me the tongue of the learned, that I should know how to speak a word in season to him that is weary. He wakeneth morning by morning. He wakeneth mine ear to hear as the learned. (Isaiah 50:4 KJV)

As I found my heart in such distress, I left the presence of the comfort of my bed. The physical suffering and emotions that overcame me were pure torment. The unbearable loss of my two children not living with me was more than I could bear.

I was sobbing, "I am sorry. I am sorry. If I knew the outcome, I never would have left your dad. I never dreamed I would be without you, Wolfgang and Hanna. The pain is awful."

I missed the two terribly. That early morning, I could not sleep. I realized that if I didn't get up, I may miss a very important time with the Lord. I went into the peach room and, falling on the floor, began to weep like a river. Such grief came all over me. Such sorrow drove the very breath from me. It was as if a whirlwind were present and continued to sweep an overwhelming feeling of emotions with such a strong, steady force that was not containable. I was shedding and shedding multiple tears, tearfully weeping!

> Thou tellest my wanderings. Put thou my tears into thy
> bottle. Are they not in thy book? (Psalms 56:8 KJV)

Then a still small voice called out, "Abigail, Abigail!"
"Yes?" I answered as I was sobbing.
"Who am I?"
"I hope you are God."
"I am, and I see your pain, and I know all things. You have done all you know to do. Now stand back. I am fighting your battles for you."
I immediately felt like a ton of bricks were lifted from me. I immediately had peace.

The Lord shall fight for you, and ye shall hold your peace. (Exodus 14:14 KJV)

These are promises He has given, and I still stand by them. I have not gotten completion yet. But I know that He has made the promise. I will stand firm. However, years had gone by, and I still didn't have my children back. I just knew that night that they were coming home. I thought they were coming back right away. I figured that was what He had meant when He made the promise. I knew doubt does not work in the kingdom of God, and I could feel doubt wanted to creep in. But I was resisting and telling the Lord, "Please don't let the doubt enter my heart. I know I heard your promise."

I just made some muffins and took them out of the oven. I had recently, at the time, gone to the doctor, and I was told that my cholesterol was high and that I was going to need to take medicine to bring it down.

I said, "Let me try to change my diet first."

The doctor said, "This is very serious, and if you can't reverse it in thirty days, you will have to take the cholesterol-lowering pills."

The boys sat patiently, waiting to go home.

I gathered them up, and I asked, "Would you like to help me make some yummy homemade muffins when we get home? My mommy and I would make these yummy muffins when I was a little girl. We would make such a huge batch that we would Tupperware them and freeze them for another day, and we can do the same. If you'd like one for a snack or for breakfast, I'll just pop one in the microwave for a bit for you. It's as close to being fresh as you can get."

Of course, this was music to their little ears and tummies. I always enjoyed helping with cooking growing up, and I wanted my children to have the same memories to look back on one day. Once the batter was finished and the first were going into the oven, the boys would run off to play with excitement, coming back in to check on them here and there, waiting for the words to flow from my mouth: "They're *ready!* Hot muffins from the oven!" Seeing the boys' faces was always a special treat for me as the muffins gave off an aroma, filling the house with baked goods. It was more than they could take.

I was telling the boys how healthy they were and how these muffins were going to hopefully help Mommy get better. Either way, we were making memories, and on top of that, there ain't nothin' like hot muffins right out of the oven with a slice of real butter. Yummy!

CHAPTER 64

Refuse Doubt

I started my chores, and I was finishing up the laundry, folding towels. I was walking down the hall to put the towels in the bathroom. As I walked, I thought about my other children and how I wished they were with us, having a hot muffin.

I was beginning to doubt the Lord. I cringed and literally forced the thought of doubt out of my mind. Why did I feel so strongly about doubt? First off, the Word says that doubt is like a ship being tossed in the wind and waves. It is good for nothing except more problems, but the Lord can't work off doubt. You have to believe even when all looks impossible. But I serve a God of the impossible because *nothing* is impossible to him who *believes*. I was thinking, *Abigail, you can't doubt. You have to believe what He said is true.*

> But let him ask in faith, nothing wavering. For he that wavereth is like a wave of the sea driven with the wind and tossed. For let not that man think that he shall receive any thing of the Lord. A double-minded man is unstable in all his ways. (James 1:6–8 KJV)

I had to dismiss the doubt immediately because it was not from the Lord. *He cannot tell a lie,* I was telling myself, which is absolutely true. I know I heard Him clearly.

Then as I passed the television, *The 700 Club* was on. Terry Anne Meeuwsen Friedrich was talking and immediately stopped her conversation and said, "The Lord just gave me a word of knowledge." She looked into the camera lens and said, "The Lord wants me to say there is a lady who just made muffins, and she told her boys how healthy they are."

I stopped in my tracks and sat at the edge of the bed with the folded towels on my lap and listened.

God said, "Who am I? I see your pain, and I know all things. You have done everything you know to do. Now stand on the Word of God and see that I am fighting your battles for you."

These were the exact sentences that God had spoken to me that night in my peach living room on the lake. I was floored, shocked, and extremely grateful. I was so thrilled that God had taken the time to share this with me in that moment. Seriously, I was thinking of doubt yet trying to rebuke it when it tried to creep in, and He came through a lady over the television. Wow! How special He is!

He did bring my son Wolfgang back to live with us in 2000 thanks to his precious sister filling me in on the details of all the evil taking place. Within one year of moving to his father's, his life fell completely apart. He ended up running away, and we were told that he snuck out a bedroom window. That was what the police report said. That did not happen because those windows have been nailed. During an investigation, he came forward, and we learned that he was being mistreated and not getting along well at all with his new stepmother. But it took what seemed to be forever when it was a little while.

The battle is still not over. He is still fighting on my behalf for my children and grandchildren. Hallelujah! I am waiting.

CHAPTER 65

God Provides Bigger Than We Could Think

The next big thing happened. Our hearts were stirring. We were not happy with the school situation and really didn't have the money to move to a different area.

> But if any provide not for his own and specially for those
> of his own house, he hath denied the faith and is worse than an
> infidel. (1 Timothy 5:8 KJV)

In fact, we talked about buying a stock, and we did, but it headed in a downward tailspin. It was losing so bad, which made us just sick. I came home and found my husband in a fetal position on the floor next to his leather chair. I will never forget that day. I knew that he was even suicidal. Believe it or not, I immediately knew in my spirit that this could only mean one thing.

I stood over him immediately and said, "First off, you cannot take your life. It doesn't belong to you."

"What?"

"You know that your body is the temple of the Holy Spirit, and you are not your own. You were bought with a price. You don't own yourself. Therefore, get up and live. He will protect you and keep you safe. You have to trust the Lord and not yourself. You say you are a Christian? Life can be hard. But you are walking through the valley of death. Yet in it, you shall fear no evil. For He is here right now. Second, this is great news to me."

He just lay there. I was standing there, looking at him.

The good news flashed all over me and said, "God has something He wants to give us, and it is right around the corner. The enemy knows it and does not want us to have it. Why? That way, God *will not* get the glory."

The word *glory* is used 148 times in Genesis, Exodus, Leviticus, and Numbers and from Deuteronomy to Malachi. The Bible tells us God clearly demonstrates His own love toward us through Him dying and returning to save us while we were yet sinners. Christ died for us. He was nailed to the cross. Now the power of sin can't harm you, and Satan loses. He no longer has power or authority. Christ made a show of those evildoers once and for all. Now we can live. Can I get an Amen? Hallelujah!

> For thou shalt worship no other god, for the Lord, whose
> name is Jealous, is a jealous God. (Exodus 34:14 KJV)

We must trust Him and turn to Him always. I told my husband, "Why don't we pray about our situation and petition the Lord and just tell Him our concerns for the boys and that we would like His help in this situation and thank Him for the solution?"

We did just that. We prayed. I really thought the prayer was authentic and real, not self-seeking. I felt the motive was pure. If one lies kicked and beaten, do you help? Absolutely. That is actually where he was, beaten down. God was getting ready to go way beyond what we could imagine. He was going to bless us and show His grace, mercy, and love toward us in a beautiful way. The hearts were pure, and He opened heaven for us. He can do the same for you.

The parable of the good Samaritan is a parable told by Jesus in the Gospel of Luke. It's about a traveler who is stripped of everything—money, clothing—beaten, and left literally half dead along this (certain) road that was known for travel for church purposes. First, a priest came. Hmmm. Then a Levite passed by. They were the very ones who were in charge of worship in the church and had all their needs met by the church so they could concentrate on the music. Really? Not one could help. Both failed miserably to meet his needs. Why? Because they were headed to church and had no time, or they would be late. Oh my goodness! Finally, a man of God arrived, a man who understood that Jesus would not pass him without first helping. We know him as the good Samaritan, who happens upon the traveler and who helps get him up. He clothed him, took him to seek medical attention, and gave money for his care. Wow! We are called to edify the weak, for in that, Christ is made strong. Oh, glory!

> Be careful for nothing, but in everything, by prayer and
> supplication with thanksgiving, let your requests be made
> known unto God. (Philippians 4:6 KJV)

God granted our unselfish prayer. We went to bed one night, and I awoke suddenly at around 4:00 a.m. I could not sleep.

I woke my husband and said, "I feel like it is Christmas morning and I want to run in the other room and open my presents." Problem was it was March.

I sat up in bed, wide awake. I could not shake it. It would not leave me. I told my husband to get up and check on the stock in Germany. The time zone would allow that. He got up and turned on the computer and sat in a daze in the chair, just stared in a trancelike state. He literally did not move.

He mumbled, "The stock I bought is at blank millions."

He just stared. We had to wait for the market to open. When the bell rang, he didn't sell right away. The stock started to drop.

He said, "I am just going to wait for it to come back up."

It kept dropping and dropping. I rolled my eyes and thought, *Are you kidding me right now? Can you say greed?* He finally sold it. We were made multimillionaires overnight, just like that. Wow! He wondered later why the stock had taken off and run so high and why the stock had dropped shortly after the opening bell.

You are never going to believe this, but this is how amazing God truly is. He confused the people by one letter. Investors *were not* supposed to be buying the very stock that we owned that had been going south for days, and we were losing money big time. Then suddenly, the Lord confused the buyers. He turned it all around. It was going up and up while we slept, turning this stock that we owned into money, simply by making sure the buyers bought a stock. They didn't even mean to buy by a letter. Everyone seemed to want that investment that night. Wow!

When the investors realized they were buying the wrong stock, the selling began, and then it started to drop in price. My husband did not sell it right away, so we did lose the original amount in the opening of the bell. But God had moved in a mysterious way on our family's behalf. I was seriously praising Jesus.

We were able to meet all our needs and then some. Our prayers had been answered in just weeks. We tithed, paid our taxes, and moved to a great town for the schools. We looked for a home, found one, and bought it, all new. We kept the lake house though. God had gone way beyond our expectations—total restoration and beyond. Notice that I had an expectation. I knew something was going to come from all this bad the day I came home and saw him on the floor. God will get all the glory, but Satan was telling my husband the opposite.

Daniel, in the Bible, had an expectation in his vision that disturbed him so much that he couldn't eat for three weeks. He waited on communication in any form from the heavenly host to help him. In his great sorrow, he was even having trouble breathing. Listen. Pray to have ears to hear. Expectations come. This is an amazing story.

In the third year of Cyrus, king of Persia, a thing was revealed unto Daniel, whose name was called Belteshazzar, and the thing was true, but the time appointed was long, and he understood the thing and had understanding of the vision. In those days, I, Daniel, was mourning three full weeks. I ate no pleasant bread. Neither came flesh nor wine in my mouth. Neither did I anoint myself at all till three whole weeks were fulfilled. And in the four-and-twentieth day of the first month, I was by the side of the great river, which is Hiddekel. Then I lifted up mine eyes and looked and beheld a certain man clothed in linen, whose loins were girded with fine gold of Uphaz. His body also was like the beryl—beryl is a mineral, usually green but also blue, rose, white, and golden and both opaque and transparent, the latter variety including the gems emerald and aquamarine, the principal ore of beryllium—and his face had the appearance of lightning and his eyes as lamps of fire and his arms and his feet like in color to polished brass and the voice of his words like the voice of a multitude. And I, Daniel, alone saw the vision, for the men that were with me saw not the vision, but a great quaking fell upon them so that they fled to hid themselves. Therefore, I was left alone and saw this great vision, and there remained no strength in me, for my comeliness was turned in me into corruption, and I retained no strength. Yet heard I the voice of his words, and when I heard the voice of his words, then was I in a deep sleep on my face and my face toward the ground. And behold—a hand touched me, which set me upon my knees and upon the palms of my hands. And he said unto me, "O Daniel, a man greatly beloved, understand the words that I speak unto thee and stand upright, for unto thee am I now sent." And when he had spoken this word unto me, I stood trembling. Then said he unto me, "Fear not, Daniel, for from the first day that thou didst set thine heart to understand and to chasten thyself before thy God, thy words were heard, and I am come for thy words."

Oh my gosh! Daniel's words are heard, and he goes on to tell him, "I am here because of your words." Wow! I love it. Daniel does not let go of what he saw and heard. The angel Michael is assuring Daniel that God heard him with his heart. Michael, the chief angel, literally taps Daniel on the knees and palms. Daniel says, "What took you so long to get here?" Michael explains to Daniel that for twenty-one days, he fought the unseen world to get to Daniel. Wow!

But the prince of the kingdom of Persia withstood me one and twenty days, but lo, Michael, one of the chief princes, came to help me, and I remained there with the kings of Persia. Now I am come to make thee understand what shall befall thy people in the latter days. [This vision that had caused such horror in Daniel's heart and mind was not for his people of his time but for the end of time, for the vision was for many days.] And when he had spoken such words unto me, I set my face toward the ground, and I became dumb. And behold, one like the similitude of the sons of men touched my lips. Then I opened my mouth and spake and said unto him that stood before me, "O my lord, by the vision, my sorrows are turned upon me, and I have retained no strength. For how can the servant of this my lord talk with this my lord?" [As for me, straight away, there remained no strength in me. Neither was there breath left in me.] Then there came again and touched me one like the appearance of a man, and he strengthened me and said, "O man greatly beloved, fear not. Peace be unto thee, be strong, yea, be strong." And when he had spoken unto me, I was strengthened and said, "Let my lord speak, for thou hast strengthened me." Then said he, "Knowest thou wherefore I come unto thee?" And now will I return to fight with the prince of Persia, and when I am gone forth, lo, the prince of Grecia shall come. But I will see thee that is noted in the scripture of truth, and there is none that holdeth with me in these things but Michael, your prince. (Daniel 10:1–21 KJV)

Now unto him that is able to do exceeding abundantly above all that we ask or think, according to the power that worketh in us, unto him be glory in the church by Christ Jesus throughout all ages, world without end. Amen. (Ephesians 3:20–21 KJV)

Rejoice evermore. Pray without ceasing. In everything, give thanks, for this is the will of God in Christ Jesus concerning you. (1 Thessalonians 5:16–18 KJV)

Now comes the interesting part. Remember one of the reasons we prayed was for the need of money to help our family. God hates debt. I knew that, and I felt that the enemy did not want us to receive the things the Lord had for us. We have to stand our ground and confess with the mouth what we are believing and know that the Lord has only good and perfect gifts for us.

That if thou shalt confess with thy mouth the Lord Jesus and shalt believe in thine heart that God hath raised him from the dead, thou shalt be saved. For with the heart, man believeth unto righteousness, and with the mouth, confession is made unto salvation. For the scripture saith, "Whosoever believeth on him shall not be ashamed. For there is no difference between the Jew and the Greek, for the same Lord over all is rich unto all that call upon him. For whosoever shall call upon the name of the Lord shall be saved. How then shall they call on him in whom they have not believed? And how shall they believe in him of whom they have not heard? And how shall they hear without a preacher? And how shall they preach, except they be sent?" as it is written. How beautiful are the feet of them that preach the gospel of peace and bring glad tidings of good things! But they have not all obeyed the gospel. For Esaias saith, "Lord, who hath believed our report?" So then faith cometh by hearing and hearing by the word of God. But I say, "Have they not heard? Yes, verily, their sound went into all the earth and their words unto the ends of the world." (Romans 10:9–18 KJV)

CHAPTER 66

Paid in Full and then Some

Testimony time—but isn't that what I am doing? Jesus made the way so we could put the children in a great school. We were elated, to say the least.

The day we met the realtor at the home we had chosen, he pulled out some paperwork, and his manner of speech was sorta trembling, yet he got the courage to ask my husband, Nabal, "You are able to write a check for the full amount?"

"We'll pay this house in full."

You could tell that he was so blown away and wondered what that feeling was like and plainly and boldly asked, "*Wow!* What is it like? I mean, how does it feel to know at this moment that you could write a check for the full amount? To pay it off completely before even moving in? And you plan on doing just that? How does that feel?"

I knew God had just opened the door for the glory of the testimony. As Christians, we want to share what Jesus has done for us. Why? Because He can do the same for you. ♥ I waited to see if my husband was going to answer the question, and he did.

First, he chuckled and giggled and said, "It's great."

He started to write down the dollar amount. Then as he was writing, he proceeded to tell the realtor that he had a system in the stock market, and it was such a great system that it was like a dump truck pulling up with a backhoe full of money, just dumping money into my dump truck, and I would drive off and go straight to the bank and do it all over again.

I listened in shock. I knew we were in trouble at that very moment. I had to give God the glory and the credit. I walked over to the realtor and told him, "First off, God is no respecter of persons. What He has done for us, He can do for you."

Then Peter opened his mouth and said, "Of a truth, I perceive that God is no respecter of persons." (Acts 10:34 KJV)

We truly had prayer time with the Lord. We asked Him, and in the petition, we were so grateful for His protection and provision. We knew we needed His help to make it happen. It looked impossible, but remember, we serve a mighty God who does the impossible. Oh, hallelujah! We placed a vision board in our hearts. It was written on the heart of our tablet, "Without a vision, you perish. Plan, for your plans from the heart, He wants to bring to pass (♥) because He is the very one who gave it to you in your heart in the first place."

Second, we were flat broke up to two weeks ago, wondering how things were going to work out. Prayer was where we had turned, and we fell on our knees and had a serious heart-to-heart conversation with the Lord! We asked him to intervene on our behalf, and we thanked him for His help for renewing us. "The enemy does not want us to have what you have for us and would want us to lose faith and confess from our mouths that it is over." My husband could not go on. He lacked *hope*. Our confession was God had something to give, and it was around the corner, and the enemy did not want us to know because God would get the glory.

Hope deferred maketh the heart sick, but when the desire cometh, it is a tree of life. Whoso despiseth the word shall be destroyed, but he that feareth the commandment shall be rewarded. The law of the wise is a fountain of life, to depart from the snares of death. (Proverbs 13:12–14 KJV)

Though I speak with the tongues of men and of angels and have no charity, I am become as sounding brass or a tinkling cymbal. And though I have the gift of prophecy and understand all mysteries and all knowledge, and though I have all faith so that I could remove mountains and have not charity, I am nothing. And though I bestow all my goods to feed the poor and though I give my body to be burned and have not charity, it profiteth me nothing. Charity suffereth long and is kind. Charity envieth not. Charity vaunteth not itself, is not puffed up, doth not behave itself unseemly, seeketh not her own, is not easily provoked, thinketh no evil, rejoiceth not in iniquity but rejoiceth in the truth, beareth all things, believeth all things, hopeth all things, endureth all things. Charity never faileth, but whether there be prophecies, they shall fail. Whether there be tongues, they shall cease. Whether there be knowledge, it shall vanish away. For we know in part, and we prophesy in part. But when that which is perfect comes, that which is in part shall be done away. When I was a child, I spake as a child. I understood as a child. I thought as a child. But when I became a man, I put away childish things. For now we see through a glass, darkly, but then face to face. Now I know in part, but then shall I know even as also I am known. And now abideth faith, hope, charity, these three, but the greatest of these is charity. (1 Corinthians 13:1–13 KJV)

For this cause, I, Paul, the prisoner of Jesus Christ for you Gentiles, say, "If ye have heard of the dispensation of the grace of God which is given me to you, how that, by revelation, he made known unto me the mystery (as I wrote afore in few words, whereby, when ye read, ye may understand my knowledge in the mystery of Christ), which, in other ages, was not made known unto the sons of men as it is now revealed unto his holy apostles and prophets by the Spirit, that the Gentiles should be fellow heirs and of the same body and partakers of his promise in Christ by the gospel, whereof I was made a minister, according to the gift of the grace of God given unto me by the effectual working of his power unto me, who is less than the least of all saints, is this grace given, that I should preach among the Gentiles the unsearchable riches of Christ and to make all men see what is the fellowship of the mystery, which, from the beginning of the world, hath been hid in God, who created all things by Jesus Christ, to the intent that now unto the principalities and powers in heavenly places might be known by the church the manifold wisdom of God, according to the eternal purpose which he purposed in Christ Jesus our Lord, in whom we have boldness and access with confidence by the faith of him. Wherefore I desire that ye faint not at my tribulations for you, which is your glory. For this cause, I bow my knees unto the Father of our Lord Jesus Christ, of whom the whole family in heaven and earth is named, that he would grant you, according to the riches of his glory, to be strengthened with might by his Spirit in the inner man, that Christ may dwell in your hearts by faith, that ye, being rooted and grounded in love, may be able to comprehend with all saints what is the breadth and length and depth and height and to know the love of Christ, which passeth knowledge, that ye might be filled with all the fullness of God. Now unto him that is able to do exceeding abundantly above all that we ask or think, according to the power that worketh in us, unto him be glory in the church by Christ Jesus throughout all ages, world without end. Amen." (Ephesians 3:1–21 KJV)

I understood you to be the one who created all things for our inheritance and that you are the God above all gods. You seek our happiness and desire to love us like no other can. God used me at that moment to bring the living waters of hope to my husband, who lay with such distress. I was not going to let the enemy win. We declare that we are nothing without you, but the glorious news is that you are the one who gives and takes away. Lord Jesus, you made the way. You died and gave us life if we chose. We have a free will to exercise and come boldly to your throne. You are so great that you would not have it any other way. You want the heart to choose. You do not force your love. Oh, we desperately need you and plead with much humility and humbleness of sincere hearts. Who would desire anything less? You, Father, literally heard our prayer and answered it. Hallelujah to the King!

> If a son shall ask bread of any of you that is a father, will he give him a stone? Or if he ask a fish, will he give fish or a serpent. Or if he shall ask an egg, will he offer him a scorpion. If ye then, being evil, know how to give good gifts unto your children, how much more shall your heavenly Father give the Holy Spirit to them that ask him? (Luke 11:11–13 KJV)
> And he said unto me, "My grace is sufficient for thee, for my strength is made perfect in weakness. Most gladly, therefore, will I rather glory in my infirmities, that the power of Christ may rest upon me." (2 Corinthians 12:9 KJV)
> But thou shalt remember the Lord thy God, for it is he that giveth thee power to get wealth, that he may establish his covenant which he swore unto thy fathers, as it is this day. And it shall be, if thou do at all forget the Lord thy God and walk after other gods and serve them and worship them, I testify against you this day that ye shall surely perish. As the nations which the Lord destroyeth before your face, so shall ye perish because ye would not be obedient unto the voice of the Lord your God. (Deuteronomy 8:18–20 KJV)

Oh my . . . What just happened? This was very serious. There was no testimony of what God had done in our lives. It was a self-credited testimony of my husband's part and what he did. Oh no. Oh no. He didn't just say that. Well, with all that said, I hope you followed what I just said. The realtor left. My husband was very upset with me for saying what I did. He had an awful look in his eyes that could burn a hole in me or turn me into a pillar of salt if I looked back. He absolutely had nothing nice to say.

I said, "Nabal, I knew that God opened a door, and if I did not give God the credit, I knew that I would be useless to Him. And I knew God had given it, and we must boost in Him. I was going to give my testimony." Then I asked, "Do you like roller coasters?"

He said, "No."

I said, "Neither do I. But you'd better put on your seatbelts because we are going for a ride, and it is not going to be fun."

Sure enough, the ride was long, hard, and very difficult—ten years and counting. I could certainly tell lots of stories within those years as well. He gave the power to receive the wealth. He had the power to take it as quickly as He had given it. It was a matter of time, and I knew it. He literally laughed at me and didn't give it a second thought. Oh no. Trouble was coming. God is a jealous God, and He just moved mountains for us.

Shortly after all that was said, my husband came and said, "I don't need God anymore. I have everything I need. I don't even have to work."

I said nothing. I was hurt and shocked, and I sat back and prayed. I knew we would suffer.

CHAPTER 67

With Just the Thought of Moving, God Provides

I had not heard from the voice in a while. Nothing. Raising the children and being a mom was where I put my heart and energy. The greatest thing ever to me is being a mother. I loved being with my children—riding bikes, baking chocolate chip cookies, watching movies, growing vegetables, tumbling rocks, going to the park, bike riding, reading, rollerblading, swimming, playing baseball, camping in the yard, going to baseball games. You name it, we did it.

I was surrounded by boys. The whole house was boys. I was the only girl. Hump! I got the idea that I would like another child, but this time, I wanted a girl, a girl whom I could dress up in froufrou all the way, a girly girl. *Yeah! We could just be girls.* Remember, I was getting too old to have babies, according to the medical protocol. The doctor asked back several pregnancies to do an amino test for possible problems.

I said, "And if there is—which there won't—what should we do? Doctor, even if I will not, so we are good to continue on, I am not invading my child's privacy."

He never asked again. I had two more children even after that last conversation with the doctor. I wanted a girl. In fact, twin girls would have been awesome. Well, I remember going into the very large bathroom where the very large mirrors were and sitting on my very large vanity shelf up close to the mirror, and stared deep into my eyes reflecting back at me. I had the most serious face—deep, real deep—and prayed, looking deep into the mirror down to the very depths of my soul.

"God, I have to have a girl. I know there is no promise of a girl, and I know health is the most important part of having a child, but please. I need a girl. And if you could, twin girls would be really great. The end. Amen!"

Well, I got pregnant. Now I was having a girl or a boy or, better yet, twin girls. Yay! I waited. Months went by, and it was time for an ultrasound. Hopefully, I would find out. The nurse announced that I was having a girl. I looked over at her, and I was so thrilled that I asked her again for sure.

I was so excited that I said, "You are sure, right?"

"Yes, I am sure."

Oh, the joy this child had given me! Praise you, Jesus! She was my comfort in one of my darkest moments. Now that was why I felt so blessed. I was literally thrown to the world, and she was there in her most precious ways to bring comfort in the tiniest of things. Just seeing her face flooded me with a warmth of love that is not expressed to its fullness. I do recall praising Jesus for the gift of her precious tiny self. ♥ You, Father, certainly know what you are doing way before we can know. I am so in love with you.

We decided to sell the home we had bought a few years back because we realized we did not need the school system and decided to homeschool. The taxes were high to live in that home. I could use that money for something else. God provided a buyer without even putting the house on the market. I was touching up the windows around back and overheard a conversation in the backyard of a middle-aged couple looking at the house next door that was on the market. I poked my head over the fence and started a conversation with them.

"Hello. My name is Abigail. Y'all are looking to buy a home?"

"Yes, we are, but this one needs a lot of work. And really, we are quite surprised it is a new house. They did not put high-end appliances in either. The homeowners did not keep it up."

"Oh, I am sorry to hear that. Our home will be up for sale soon, if you would like to look at it."

"Oh, wow! Thanks for letting us know. However, we are booked for the day with a lot of homes to look at."

"No worries. I am a stay-at-home mom. Please feel free to come look at ours when you can. I will be happy to show you the house. But before you make a decision, please come and look. It is a lovely home, and it is in excellent condition and has high-end appliances."

Then we said our goodbyes. A few days later, there was a knock at the door, and it was them, and it was sold. Wow! God is so perfect.

CHAPTER 68

Your House Is Going on Sale in May

We moved back to the lake house. We really enjoyed the area we were living in and really had a hard time adjusting at the lake. We really wanted to move back to the area we had just left. One day my husband was out of town and found a brand-new neighborhood. The house we choose was under construction. We were able to pick and choose everything we wanted in the home.

He said, "I would like for you to see this neighborhood."

We went and fell in love. We decided to homeschool in the large day basement. It was perfect. The room was big, and each child had their own desk, with dividing walls that were movable for privacy. The glass French doors that opened to the huge backyard were comforting from the schoolroom. We also had a grand playground just literally down the street, and we went quite often. God is good. He provides all this.

I hadn't heard from my still small voice, nothing. Then one day we were all piling up in the car to go to the library. We loved reading. Just weeks before, the Lord pointed it out to me—and it stood out and was so interesting, to say the least—and this is what was said: "The wood in houses cry out to the heavens if you do not belong in them."

"What? The wood cries out?"

He went on to say, "Anything that is not earned is stolen, and the stolen item cries out to me." This was a wow moment to me, and in a flash, the voice said, "The housing market is going to crash."

I did not know how or when, but I knew it was going to crash. I just knew that it was going to crash but did not know the timing.

"Get out! Sell your home!"

There was such an urgency in my voice as I told Nabal Suka. I was just trying to get in the car and sit down, and as I was in motion, I heard and saw everything clearly before I even sat down in the car. That's how quick it was. It was like I saw panicking and scrambling in the nation, and then I heard the words again.

"Get out! Sell your home!"

At the time, we had only been in the home for one year. It was brand new. It was around 4,500 square feet finished and another 1,400 unfinished, just a beautiful Georgian-style home.

I turned and looked at my husband and said, "We have to sell the house. The Lord showed me that something terrible is going to happen to the housing market. I don't know exactly what that is, but we have to get out." I immediately thought, *Only a crazy woman is going to look her husband in the eye and say, "We have to sell our brand-new house."*

He said, "Okay?" to my surprise.

We put the house up for sale. Months went by, and there were no buyers, nothing. I thought, *I know I heard you, Father. If you are in this and you said to sell, which I know you did, what is happening? What is it. Why has it not sold? I don't understand.* I woke up one morning scooted over to the edge of the bed. My feet were literally dangling off the side. This bed was so massive that you had to jump to get on it.

All I was thinking about was a cup of coffee when all of a sudden, I heard, "Your house is going to sell in May!"

I went into the kitchen and said, "I am just putting this out there, but I heard the house will sell in May."

Now whether it would sell or not is a different story. That was it. May came, and it only had two days left. The phone rang, and it was a realtor wanting to make an appointment for a looker.

I said, "Yes, of course."

They came that afternoon and looked. I got a call back on the last day of May, and I was told, "She loves your home. And one other in a completely different neighborhood. She wants to look one last time. I will get back with you this afternoon because she said she will be buying one of the two homes she chooses today."

"Sure, of course."

I already knew she would be buying the home. I went to the park down the street and thanked the Lord. Well, it was getting late, and I saw that she was at a home right down the street from ours that just went on the market the very same day, May 31. I mentioned to Nabal that I saw the buyers looking at the neighbor's house that just come up for sale today.

"Do you think she got sidetracked and wants it?"

"Yes, I think she wants the other house. She is still at the neighbor's house, looking."

"What?"

The phone rang about this time. It was the realtor, and she was thanking for showing the house. "She absolutely loved your home. But as we drove in, she noticed another home that just came on the market in your neighborhood, and she wanted to take a look and have a final decision. She was going to buy your home. But the last look at the last minute changed her mind. I am sorry."

"Wow . . . I don't understand. I know I heard God's voice." *Back to square one. I do recall talking to the Lord. Why? Was I too cocky? Did I do something wrong?* I was truly sorry.

Months went by—and no buyers, nothing. I thought, *I know I heard you, Father. If you are in this and you said to sell, which I know you did, then what am I doing wrong?* Three months had gone by, and we still owned the house, with no buyers yet. *What is going on? I don't understand?*

This was very sad news indeed. News was spreading that one early morning a neighbor was killed in a car wreck on her way to work. I found out the details of who it was, and my heart gripped me with complete sadness. I remember going into another room to talk to the Lord. *Oh, God, she is the one who looked at our home and almost bought it. She has three young children. One is just three months old. Oh, God, this is awful. She just gave birth to a baby boy. He will never know his mother and her two younger daughters. Oh, my heart hurts for this family. The children and their father's grief has to be so overwhelming.*

As I was feeling the pain and anguish for the family's loss. I heard these words very clearly. There was no way I could've thought this. "Abigail, it's better to be obedient than to sacrifice."

"What? I don't understand."

I heard these words. "Had she bought your house, she never would have been in that spot. The distance from your house to the wreck would have made all the difference for the wreck, and it never would have happened."

"What? The distance never would have put her there? The timing made the difference? Oh, my God! That is awful. God, are you telling me that she knew that she was supposed to buy our home and got sidetracked? Did she have the voice of the Holy Spirit too? Oh, God, I am so sad for her and her family."

I never heard an answer to that question, but I do think that she did. Why else would the Father tell me that it was better to be obedient than to sacrifice? I refused to call the house home, and we packed up and moved back to the awful lake house. I went right to work, ripping out old sheet rock and doing whatever I could to make it livable.

CHAPTER 69

Search Your Hearts

No sooner when I said this, I was asked, "Search your heart and see if something is blocking it." So I did. I really got nothing, *nothing*. I thought about it for days—nothing. Then I was told, "Go to your husband and ask him to search his heart to see if there is anything on his part." I went and asked him.

He immediately said, "No, nothing. I don't have anything."

I said, "You need to search. I am not looking for an immediate answer," and I left the thought with him.

Days later, he came to me and said, "I've got it."

I said, "Got what?"

"The answer. The answers to your question. I knew that I wasn't supposed to buy this house. I was not even supposed to buy this house." He hung his head.

"Oh my goodness! What are you talking about?"

He continued to say, "You were having a baby, and I know you didn't want to live in the lake house that had fallen apart. It was left abandoned for over seven long years. It was molding, and everything needed redoing. I also remembered why you wanted to sell the house. I know you wanted to come back to relieve us from the expensive taxes. We could afford it, but you said you could think of a million other uses for the tax money. I agreed, but I also knew the lake house was a mess. But God provided a buyer straight away *without* a realtor, just through a conversation that you had with buyers looking next door. And it sold. But you were pregnant, and I knew you would want to do the work on fixing the lake house, but that was not realistic at that moment. I also knew how much you loved the other area, even though we went back to the lake house, and the situation wasn't good. And then one day I found a new neighborhood while you were home and called, and we looked, and we bought it. I do recall how nice it was to move to the Hollies—new, clean, and just perfect for a brand-new beautiful baby girl."

"What? What are you saying?" I sat and stared into the space that surrounded me and said, "God told you not to buy this home? And you did anyway?" I knew in a flash that this was the reason why the house was not selling. "We've got to ask God to forgive us. Oh my . . . You should not put me above God. He is first."

But I also thought about the voice that said it would in May. I was shocked and surprised with his answer, but it made sense. I thought that it was so true, everything he had said. The lake house was awful and needed a ton of work. With a baby just days away, that just could not happen, and the mold—oh my! You were working hard to get rid of the crap. It was awful. *We can't have children in this house. How can we continue to live here?* I certainly understood where he was coming from. We got down on our knees, and we prayed and asked the Lord to forgive us, sincerely prayed.

Within two weeks, we met a woman named Naomi Rahab, who happened to be a widow. (I called her Naomi Rahab, the widow woman who sustained us. Hallelujah!) Naomi had lost her sons and her husband. She had two daughters-in-law, and out of that, Ruth went back with Naomi to her people to find food and shelter. Naomi was an Israelite who believed in God, but she had a very bitter life. She had to go back to her people, and Ruth went with her.

Rahab, in case you do not know, is found in the Book of Joshua. She lived in Jericho, which is the Promised Land. The city was going to be captured by Jacob and Caleb, the only two who had led the Israelites and believed that God was with them and could conquer the city. Rahab was a prostitute, which I find interesting because the lineage of Jesus comes from her. It just goes to show you how God can use anyone, even prostitutes. He loves you. Rahab hid these two men inside her walls, and her family and herself were spared. The rest died. It is a great read. Read the story. The Israelites captured the city by hiding two men who had been sent to reconnoiter the city. God really has a sense of humor. He is awesome. God sent a widow named Naomi Rahab. Really? Wow! He has such a sense of good, loving humor.

The house closed. Naomi Rahab entered the closing sale with her realtor. The room literally filled my heart with gladness for the Lord to provide this wonderful woman to buy our home.

I said, "I could just kiss you!" (I probably should not have said that, but it just came out of my mouth). I wondered, *What the heck did a widow need with such a massive house?* I quickly dismissed it and was glad God had sent her.

The very next day—I wish I were kidding—the headlines read, "Jumbo interest only loans default." The housing market started plummeting, literally cut in half. Builders went out of business. Large homes were unfinished and left abandoned. Wow! God had shown me a crash in the housing twenty-two months earlier, yet I had no idea that people living in their homes were only paying interest on them. What? You are kidding!

I flashed back to a fact I had read in the Bible months before I got the vision and knowledge was given about the housing problem. Remember, I did not know the wholeness of why. I just knew God said, "Sell!" The verse read, "If you don't belong in a house, the very wood cries out to the heavens." There were people throughout the land who did not belong in those homes.

Everything we have is a gift from the Father. It is not ours. We are taking care of His things. (Leviticus 25:23)

The earth is the Lord's and the fullness thereof, the world and those who dwell therein. (Psalm 24:1–34 ESV)

Do not envy evil people or wish you were with them because their minds plot violence, and their lips talk trouble. With wisdom, a house is built. With understanding, it is established. With knowledge, its rooms are filled with every kind of riches, both precious and pleasant. A strong man knows how to use his strength, but a person with knowledge is even more powerful. After all, with the right strategy, you can wage war, and with many advisers, there is victory. Matters of wisdom are beyond the grasp of a stubborn fool. At the city gate, he does not open his mouth. Whoever plans to do evil will be known as a schemer. Foolish scheming is sinful, and a mocker is disgusting to everyone. If you faint in a crisis, you are weak. Rescue captives condemned to death and spare those staggering toward their slaughter. When you say, "We didn't know this," won't the one who weighs hearts take note of it? Won't the one who guards your soul know it? Won't he pay back people for what they do? Eat honey, my son, because it is good. Honey that flows from the honeycomb tastes sweet. The knowledge of wisdom is like that for your soul. If you find it, then there is a future, and your hope will never be cut off. You wicked one, do not lie in ambush at the home of a righteous person. Do not rob his house. A righteous person may fall seven times, but he gets up again. However, in a disaster, wicked people fall. Do not be happy when your enemy falls, and do not feel glad when he stumbles. The LORD will see it. He won't like it, and he will turn his anger away from that person. Do not get overly upset with evildoers. Do not envy wicked people because an evil person has no future, and the lamps of wicked people will be snuffed out. Fear the LORD, my son. Fear the king as well. Do not associate with those who always insist upon change because disaster will come to them suddenly. Who knows what misery both may bring? These also are the sayings of wise people.

Showing partiality as a judge is not good. Whoever says to a guilty person, "You are innocent," will be cursed by people and condemned by nations. But people will be pleased with those who convict a guilty person, and a great blessing will come to them. Giving a straight answer is [like] a kiss on the lips. Prepare your work outside, and get things ready for yourself in the field. Afterward, build your house. Do not testify against your neighbor without a reason, and do not deceive with your lips. Do not say, "I'll treat him as he treated me. I'll pay him back for what he has done to me." I passed by a lazy person's field, the vineyard belonging to a person without sense. I saw that it was all overgrown with thistles. The ground was covered with weeds, and its stone fence was torn down. When I observed [this], I took it to heart. I saw it and learned my lesson. "Just a little sleep, just a little slumber, just a little nap." Then your poverty will come like a drifter, and your need will come like a bandit. (Proverbs 24 ESV)

The Word of God is so refreshing that it's like water that quenches the deer's thirst.

CHAPTER 70

God Shares an Awful Vision

One night, as I lay sleeping, my dream became so real that I knew the Lord was communicating the future to me. I saw Nabal running down a road. It was a long straight dark road. I clearly saw his clothing, some of which looked very familiar, a simple white T-shirt and a pair of brown boots that he always wore. But the pants were not something he would usually wear. They were brown. Now you may be asking yourself, "So? What's the big deal?" He only wears blue jeans. That has been his choice ever since I've known him.

Then suddenly, in the dream, I saw a giant ball the size of the earth rolling toward him, with flames shooting out in every direction. Inside, this massive wheel had tons of individual paisley shapes that cracked open, and eyeballs were exposed. They were packed to the brim, going in every direction. These eyeballs could see. It was so creepy!

I questioned the Lord. "I get the giant ball of fire. But I don't understand the eyeballs."

"The eyeballs are all the reminders of the evil things that he has done to intentionally hurt another human being. He will constantly review this pain caused to others by him, and he will see the wrong and know that it was wrong but will not be able to change it."

My heart immediately started to ache because I knew there were a lot of things that he had said to people to hurt them in so many ways. I was seriously grieving for him. These eyes had nothing connected to anything. They were just eyes. This is the wheel mentioned in the Bible. I called it Ezekiel's wheel.

"The eyes are gathering information of the testimony of the people on Earth who will give an account because I see all that is written with the witnesses."

"Oh, Jesus! These eyeballs are gathering information for you? These are witnesses?"

"Yes. My Son died for all sin except one, and that is denying the Holy Spirit and the power therein. All things are possible to him who will only believe. But the Holy Spirit is true and will not go outside of the truth. So what is the truth? When you find it, it will set you free. And you will no longer desire sin but live in truth. In truth, you will find perfect peace no matter what you face. And it is found in the perfect Lamb I sent. He is filled with compassion when you turn from your evil. But you must find Him while you are alive and have your being on Earth."

I didn't mention this vision to him. It wasn't good. Then one day my husband came through the front door and showed me some clothes that he had bought at Academy. When he pulled the brown pants out of the bag, I stopped everything and stared.

He asked, "What is it?" (Not really. He never would ask what was wrong. Hmmm. It just sounded good, being concerned when someone is staring.)

I told him about the vision that I had with him wearing those pants, those same brown pants. He laughed at me and didn't think anything of it. Months later, he went to go pay the water bill, which was right down the street from our house. It was like five minutes. I noticed it was getting late and he hadn't come home yet. I was thinking, *Something isn't right because it's not that far. He should be home by now.* Well, as soon as I thought this, the phone rang. It was him.

"My car is on fire!" he was screaming on the phone as he breathed heavily, with short breaths.

The first thing I asked him was "Are you out of the car yet?" From the sound of it, he was not. It was almost like he was in disbelief that his car was on fire. "Get out of the car!"

Then the phone went dead. I tried to call him back, but there was no answer. Around five minutes later, he called, and he began to tell me the story of what had taken place.

"As I left the house, everything was fine, and I was going to fill up the car with gas because it was almost empty, but then something told me not to fill the car up yet, which really isn't uncommon for me. You know how bad I am, pushing the limits on an empty tank. I continued to go to the fire station to pay the water bill. When I got to the fire station, I could not see the drop-off box. It was getting dark, but when I got out of the car, I really couldn't see. Smoke was all around me. I didn't think anything of it because I figured the fire department was having a fire drill. I swished the smoke away with my hands, and then I proceeded to crawl back in the car."

He had to crawl back in the car because the driver's door had been smashed, and it would not open—nor would the driver's window. He had been crawling out the passenger side of the vehicle, so now he was crawling back in the car with smoke all around him, and he was just thinking it was the fire department.

"As I was driving on down the road, I noticed sparks under the car, but I just figured it was my muffler dragging. I didn't check it out either. I just kept driving, and then all of a sudden, I thought, 'You know what? The car could be on fire.' So I rolled down the back and passenger windows, and when I rolled down the windows, apparently this created more oxygen to feed the flames. The next thing I knew, flames were billowing out through the cracks of the floor and dash. I immediately slammed on the breaks. The flames started to engulf the car. I crawled out and started running for my life, trying to get far away from the vehicle, where the flames were totally out of control."

I said, "Wow! Thank God you did not fill the car up with gasoline even at the gas station. You may have had a spark ignite the whole place. Not to mention there could have been a huge explosion as you were driving or when you were trying to get away from it."

There were so many possibilities that were not good in the outcome, but God protected anyone who may have been involved. See, God's provision was there, even when others knew not. He did not let him go to the gas station and fill up.

"Yes, that is true. But as I was running away from this dilapidated vehicle—it was mutilated, just a pathetic piece of junk—another man was running toward the car to put the fire out."

"What? You didn't tell him to run and not be concerned for the car?"

"No! I was too busy trying to get away!"

"You should've told him to turn around and run! The car is not worth saving!"

By this time, it was engulfed in flames, and all the man had was a tiny fire extinguisher. Thank God the car was not full of gas. That man could've died. I was praising Jesus seriously. When he walked in the door, he didn't say a word, but he had on a white T-shirt, brown pants, and the boots that were in the vision I had had months before, and he never wore those pants again.

CHAPTER 71

The Man Who Came to Blow Up My House—In a Dream, That Is

There was a knock at the door. There stood a short but handsome man with clean-cut blond hair and blue eyes. He and I talked. He mentioned he was from Germany. I loved his accent, and I was just intrigued by him in every way. He was very likable. We laughed, we talked.

Then he said, "I really like you."

"Well, thank you. I really like you as well."

He then said, "I am going to be honest with you. I am here to blow your house up."

"What?" I could tell he was very serious. He was not joking. "What? Why my house?"

"Why not your house? It is a great spot," he replied.

I stood there, staring into his eyes. He was very, very serious. "I am confused right now. I don't understand. Why are you telling me this?"

"Because I like you, and I am giving you a chance to get out of here before I blow it up."

"You're giving me a chance? A chance to leave? Oh my gosh!"

"I am leaving now. I will be back within a short time, and by the time I get back, I don't want to see you here. Do you understand?"

He left. My brain was going in a million directions. I was a frantic mess. I ran to tell my husband, if that's what I should call him, but this dream confirmed that he was not. He had left me a long time ago—spiritually, physically, emotionally, and financially. Anyhoo, I told him what had just taken place. I began to see him throwing his clothes in a bag. I was standing, looking out my picture window in my bedroom. I saw construction workers across the

175

lake, and they were busy scurrying around, building a house, and framing it up without a care in the world when all of a sudden, a man fell to his death from the roof rafters. Everyone was in horror and went running to his rescue to help him, but it was too late. I knew in my heart that he was dead, and as I looked and watched the emergency workers arrive, I thought, *Oh my goodness, all of you will be dead very soon and don't even know it. A bomb is going to go off and blow this area away.* I could not believe this was happening.

As I stood there, thinking, my husband came up from behind me and whispered in my ear, "It was nice knowing you."

I turned, and I looked at him as he walked out the door. I was in complete disbelief. Wow! Now I was running through the house, trying to find my children, screaming their names.

"Grab your stuff! We gotta get out of here quickly!"

I started to throw things in my bag, and as I was throwing things in my bag, nothing made sense. I had socks that didn't match. I started thinking about not having a bathtub to take a bath. I wasn't going to have a bed to sleep in. I wasn't going to have a soft pillow to lay my head on. *I need blankets. We are going to be sleeping while homeless.* I started thinking of all the things I wasn't going to have, and while I was stuffing my bag, nothing made sense. I didn't have anything that worked. I mean, it was ridiculous, and then I was screaming throughout the house, telling the children to hurry.

"We've gotta get out of here!"

I couldn't find them. They must have been packing. In the back of my mind, I was listening to my children. I was thinking in overload. *My husband is gone. He didn't even give a thought to his children. I wonder, what kinda life have I been living?*

Then I turned and looked. There, the man stood, staring at me. He was back, dressed in camouflage, with a giant bomb strapped to his body. *Oh my gosh! He is a suicide bomber? What?* He looked at me with a look like "You've got to be kidding me. You are still here?"

I wanted this dream over. I begged to wake up, and I did. I remember thinking, *That was awful, just awful, to know that people could be like that. We hear these stories on the news of suicide bombers. Why did I have this crazy dream, Lord?*

I asked, and He proceeded to tell me, "While you watched the young man fall to his death from the roof, many others ran to his rescue. Knowing he was already dead, you needed to tell them that the whole area was going to be blown up. You were so busy trying to get everything just right, and the more you tried to get everything you needed, the more nothing was working for you. You were so busy taking care of your needs that others were going to die because you knew something very important and did not tell them. Tell them that the enemy is lurking around, and you need to save yourself. You did nothing except try to pack clothing, and in your own chaos, nothing was getting done right. You thought of yourself, not others around you. You must warn them."

I was so conflicted. Now every time I see construction workers, I think of this dream. I have even pulled over and told them how much God loves them, and I do talk about His love for us. ♥

CHAPTER 72

The Three Yellow Circles
and the Golden Crown

It's morning here at my house. Good morning to you, my reader. The Lord's face shines on you, and He does give you peace that passes all understanding. We get to make our day great, for it is a choice.

> The Lord bless thee and keep thee. The Lord make his face shine upon thee and be gracious unto thee. The Lord lift up his countenance upon thee and give thee peace. (Numbers 6:24–26 KJV)

As I awoke this morning, my eyes caught a glimpse of three circles of shimmering golden light through the crack of my window shade—and the pleasant silhouette of a man! *Jesus, is that you?* Every hue was found as I squeezed my eyes just a bit to play with the light. It turned into long glittering rays of light shining down from the three circles that crowned the top of the head of the man, streaming down rays on his face. Whether in body or out, He was there. The light was present. The sparkling light had life. It danced down and up, returning to the three circles.

I asked myself, *What are the circles about?* My thoughts were that the light of life has every color of the rainbow. That's what makes each one unique. The three golden circles lead to the crown of life that is found at the resurrection. The luminaries shine on *all* life. Humans are His love. When one really hears with His spirit, mind, and body, He lives fully in the plan of God! When man sees, He brings comfort to all. When man hears, He acts on the truth. When man speaks, the Word of God goes forth throughout the ends of the earth, bringing benefits to grow the perfect love that is found in Him. The shadow of the pleasant silhouette of the man is His prize. He provides light, and it shines on the good and the bad.

> But I say unto you, "Love your enemies, bless them that curse you, do good to them that hate you, and pray for them which despitefully use you and persecute you, that ye may be the children of your Father which is in heaven, for he maketh his sun to rise on the evil and the good and sendeth rain on the just and on the unjust. For if ye love them which love you, what reward have ye? Do not even the publicans the same?" (Matthew 5:44–46 KJV)

He loves mankind dearly. We belong to Him. The wholeness of His heart fits perfectly into His unfailing love that He has for mankind! We are His prize. The circles—could they be the Father, Son, and Holy Ghost? The crown is everlasting life. "My rays are present and are alive. Look in the details. There is life, an amazing life in the present moment and ever after."

> Ask, and it shall be given you. Seek, and ye shall find. Knock, and it shall be opened. For everyone who asks receives, he who seeks finds, and to him who knocks, the door will be *open*. (Matthew 7:7–8)

CHAPTER 73

The House That Had Been Abandoned

We were back in the lake house, and it needed a pile of work. Have you heard the saying "A house that is not lived in falls apart"? Pretty much everything was wrong with this house. With it shut up, mold was having its way. Windows were rusting. The sheet rock had a musty smell.

> Lay not up for yourselves treasures upon the earth, where moth and rust consume and where thieves break through and steal, but lay up for yourselves treasures in heaven, where neither moth nor rust doth consume and where thieves do not break through nor steal, for where thy treasure is, there will thy heart be also. (Matthew 6:19–21 ASV)

The lake house needed work—and lots of it. We had a window company come to the house to give us a bid. All they were going to do was take out the old and put the same size back. The plan was awful, and the price was $22,000. When I heard this, I sat up to shake his hand and apologized for wasting his time.

"I am so sorry. Your time is valuable. I never should have wasted your time had I known. That price you quoted is way more money than I thought it would be."

Then to my horror, he said, "Your house is ugly."

"You are right. Why do you think I asked you about windows?" I was literally in shock. I should've reported him, but I didn't.

Meanwhile, we went to church and sat behind this man and his wife. The couple was in the business of selling new kitchen cabinets for much cheaper prices than most cabinets places, and we were in need of new ones for sure. We decided to go check it out. To our delight, he also sold windows, which we didn't know. This is how God works, perfectly and on time. Shout out praise with song!

> He has made everything beautiful in his time. Also, he has set the world in their heart so that no man can find out the work that God maketh from the beginning to the end. (Ecclesiastes 3:11 KJV)

Okay, he had some really huge windows, all vinyl, just what we wanted. Wow! Perfect again! Not wood—it rots. The windows we had were metal, and they were rusting. Yuck! Even with everything the way it was, we delighted ourselves in the Lord, and we knew in His time, He would give us the desires of our hearts. This was His promise to us. I was not letting go. Hallelujah! So here we were in a store, looking for the kitchen, and we found an amazing deal for the whole house on windows: $2,200. Remember Sears coming out and just replacing the same-sized windows, which were tiny, for $22,000? Wow! A huge thank-you, Lord! We had no idea, but He did.

CHAPTER 74

Remodeling — God Provides in Ways We Know Not

We were doing a lot of remodeling and homeschooling the boys. The house was basically torn apart. Everything was gutted. The new windows were going in, and the old insulation was ripped out. It was a mess. It was so cold that we all wore jackets in the house, and we cooked on the outside grill in the freezing cold. The cold would get your blood pumping, and the crisp air was rather pleasant. Ha . . . You were forced to feel alive, and I highly recommend it. But most of the time, we cooked on the open fireplace. Now that was fun, and I got rather creative with it.

We all slept in one area of the house, blocking out the cold with blankets that hung from the ceiling to the floor. We were able to keep at least one room warm at all times with the large fireplace, which was always ready to cook a meal on. "Why did we do that?" you ask. Because the kitchen had been gutted. Absolutely nothing was in the kitchen area. We had found some amazing kitchen appliances. One was a top-of-the-line six-burner with a serious grill. My husband mentioned wanting one. I looked online, and they were priced at $10,000 to $15,000. I told him that the only way that was going to happen was if God wanted us to have one. He would provide one—and not at those prices.

We went to a Jewish shop called Mazers, and lo and behold—as we looked for a double oven, there it was, right there in the aisle that we were walking down. In fact, it was right smack in the path and had just been delivered. I looked at the price, realizing it was cheaper than the double oven we were looking at. *Oh my gosh! God wants us to have this!* It was at $10,000, scratched and dented, and the scratches were on the side, not even visible to the eye once it was in place.

Wow! God just blows the mind if you allow Him. I can say for sure that God hears even the details. Praise goes to my Father! Hallelujah! Sing hallelujah!

The song is written on our hearts. Raise a hallelujah to God over all things! The angels hearken unto the praise. Raise hallelujah to the King! I just got excited again. Please stop and close your eyes and take a small piece of time to listen to this beautiful song: "Good Good Father" by Chris Tomlin. We are loved by you, Father. You are perfect in *all* your ways.

The appliances had been delivered to our home, yet we were not ready for them to go in.

CHAPTER 75

The Trespassers

One night, before I closed my eyes, I had a word of knowledge that something unpleasant was going to happen during the night.

> But when He, the Spirit of Truth (the Truth-giving Spirit) comes, He will guide you into all the Truth (the whole, full Truth). For He will not speak His own message [on His own authority], but He will tell whatever He hears [from the Father; He will give the message that has been given to Him], and He will announce and declare to you the things that are to come [that will happen in the future]. (John 16:13 AMP)

I was trained to know this, and I received it. I call this the word of knowledge. Obviously, prayer will change things. That was the first thing I did. When you know something, even though you may not know all of it, that is where you pray and be intuitive to know that God is bigger than anything that comes your way. I always ask for my angels to assist me and protect me.

> Be careful for nothing, but in everything, by prayer and supplication with thanksgiving, let your requests be made known unto God. And the peace of God, which passeth all understanding, shall keep your hearts and minds through Christ Jesus. (Philippians 4:6–7 KJV)
>
> Be not forgetful to entertain strangers, for thereby some have entertained angels unawares. (Hebrews 13:2 KJV)
>
> Are they not all ministering spirits, sent forth to minister for them who shall be heirs of salvation? (Hebrews 1:14 KJV)

I prayed and really didn't even want to sleep knowing this. I wasn't sure what it was. Was it going to be a house fire or unwanted house guests? I had told the boys that if the house caught on fire, we needed a plan. So we talked it over and repeated the information to one another, and I made sure they completely understood what to do, and they did. I was so unsure of the unpleasant thing that I was told was going to happen.

I also thought, *What if it was unwanted guests?* I turned to our dog, Cookie, patting and telling her, "The Lord told me an uncomfortable thing was going to happen, and when you hear with your sixth sense, you will need to warn us if anything out of the ordinary should happen."

The scriptures talk about all the beasts we have control over. This is God's promise to us.

> All the animals of the earth, all the birds of the sky, all the small animals that scurry along the ground, and all the fish in the sea will look on you with fear and terror. I have placed them in your power. (Genesis 9:2 NLT)

I loved her, patting her, and told her, "You are a good dog."

I also knew she would let us know if anything strange happened. I finally couldn't keep my eyes open for another minute, and we were all asleep. In the wee hours of the morning, my dog started to act strange. circling the bed, rubbing my hand with her nose and head, but didn't bark. Back and forth, I felt her furry body for several minutes. I woke finally and knew that she was expressing concern to me. I woke up immediately, completely. There was nothing out of the ordinary.

Then within five minutes, a car with its headlights on started to come all the way down the steep hill right to the front of our home. We had a giant window in the kitchen where there were no drapes, and the headlights were shining straight into the house. They just sat there. Time stood still, and it felt like forever. They must have been debating on what they were going to do. Whoever they were, they were not frightened of us. You could literally feel evil in the air. Of course, I called the police immediately when I saw the lights. I knew this was not a good situation. I also knew that it would take the police a while to get here if we were in trouble. It seemed we were in a standoff with the unwanted guest, who took it upon themselves with an attitude ("Just as a matter of fact, I am coming to your house in the wee hours"). It was creepy.

We turned on every light in the house, which did not make sense, but that was what we did. That did not frighten them. They just sat there in the car. This went on for some time. Then finally, they backed up the hill and left. During the remodel, we had so many people in and out of the house working that the only thing we concluded on was one of the workers had come back with a crew to our home to steal the very expensive appliances that sat wrapped in the middle of the floor. They probably could not believe that we were actually living in a torn-up house as we remodeled.

I know being armed with the information made me definitely more aware, and when the dog was acting strange, it forced me to pay attention to my surroundings. If we had not a warning, would they have gotten in the house without us knowing until it was too late? I don't know, but I think so. Why else would God warn me. I do know He did warn me hours before we were going to have an unpleasant situation. Wow! Praise you, Jesus!

I know of this story I once heard. It was so amazing that I would like to share it. One night an old woman loved the Lord with all her heart and was so attuned to hear the voice of the Lord. She got in her bed, all nice and comfortable, but she had a word of knowledge and was told to get up and put bleach in her toilet. This meant she was going to have to go to the other end of the house to get the bleach. But she knew that voice, and she did not question or argue with her knowing. (The voice is to protect you from something that is going to go wrong. Satan has plans, but Jesus will blot out his plans that are trying to bring harm.) Amen!

Anyhoo, she obeyed and did exactly that and went back to bed. She slept really great, woke up, went into her bathroom area, and lifted the toilet lid! There in the water was a dead cottonmouth. See, Satan had sent the snake to bite and possibly kill her. God knew the plan of the enemy and stopped it in its tracks. I love this provision. However, she had to act on the voice and do what it had told her to do. This is for you as well—that is, if you don't already have it.

CHAPTER 76

God Provides through Christmas Bows

Christmas was looking straight at us, and I know the Lord doesn't like debt. I had learned from a very dear friend on how to make bows years before. I had decided to make some and go door to door. I bought one roll for $12, which made quite a few. Anything after three bows was a profit. Then I would buy another roll and so on.

My son Preston was the only one who, at the time, was old enough to go with me. He wanted to go. He thought he would enjoy helping me, and we did have fun. Of course, he earned a little money to shop for Christmas gifts to give his siblings himself. He went down one side, and I went down the other. I could see him at all times. He seemed to enjoy this outing with me. He came to this one house and was asked some questions about why he was selling bows.

Preston responded, "The truth is that my mother is making the bows so we can make Christmas happen for my brothers and sisters. My mother said, 'It wouldn't be right to not have gifts under the tree on Christmas morning.'"

"Oh, that is nice!" the lady responded.

Preston came to me afterward and said that he had tried to sell the lady some bows. She gave him a $20 bill but did not take any bows and told him to sell the bows to someone else. He didn't know what to do.

As we were talking about this, the lady pulled up and said, "You are the lady selling bows, right?"

Preston tapped me and said, "Momma, that is the lady I was telling you about."

I said, "Oh." I turned and asked the woman, "You gave my son $20. You need four bows?" I walked over to her car with the four bows.

She said, "Oh, no. I wanted to tell you that my husband and I have a church here in town. Our phone is ringing off the hook right now with Christmas around the corner from parents with children who are looking for money—a handout for nothing in return. They just say we have kids, and they expect us to give them money to help, which we do. We want children to have something under a tree. But I was literally shocked when I heard what your son said. You are trying to make Christmas happen for your children."

"Please. I want to give you something." I asked repeatedly for her to take some bows in return.

She said, "Oh, no. Sell them to someone else." She handed me a folded bill.

I thanked her, and that was it. Preston and I were about to finish for the day. It was getting darker and cooler outside. As she drove off, I opened the bill and saw that it was $100. I started to praise Jesus and cried, thanking God. I was shocked, so thankful. I was shaking and thrilled.

"Preston! Look! She gave us $100 and took no bows, and she gave you a twenty at her home! Oh my goodness! God is so, so very good!"

I called my sister-in-law and told her how God had just blessed us by this woman and her mother who came looking for us in their car. I recalled the name of the church that she had mentioned her husband pastored in. I sat down that evening and quickly penned a sincere appreciation letter to the church and how they had shined the light of Jesus through the kindness of theirs actions that day. I was profusely thankful.

Well, it wasn't long, and I got a phone call from the church (that day, we had phone books, and you could find a number with the name).

The pastor's wife said, "My husband read your letter to the church. There was not a dry eye in the service, and then they started to walk up to the altar and made an offering for your family. I would like to meet you so that we can get it to you."

Christmas was perfect. We were able to have a wonderful Christmas, with gifts, a breakfast, and even a Christmas dinner. God gave way beyond I could have thought or even imagined through Christmas bows and *the* most precious lady ever who taught me how to make them many years before. I was so truly thankful for the beautiful hearts of the people who gave that year and for my dear friend who showed me many moons before how to make them in the first place. I love and adore you, my very special friend! ♥

CHAPTER 77

Using the Innocent to Get What You Want

Remember when I told my husband that we were going on a roller coaster ride? Little by little, my husband was eroding away as a man of God, a husband, and definitely a dad. By this time, I really was beginning to refuse to pray with him. Really! The reason why was every time we prayed, we were calling on the name of the Lord. We went to the heavenly throne in a prayer of thanksgiving and invoked a petition for the Lord to answer. We involved the highest God Almighty, and Nabal would make promises to God that he never kept.

God was good to answer our prayers, and Nabal knew it but never gave the glory to God. I had to stop praying with him. I felt like I was committing a crime allowing this, and at what point was I going to be accountable, yoking up with one who asked God to do something through prayer and then, when it happens, does not give God the glory? I just could no longer join in prayer. I told him so as well.

One day he came and asked me to pray about his office that we still had, which, at this point, he never went to. He had put it on the market, but it wasn't selling.

"Will you pray with me that the office would sell?" he said.

I asked him several questions. "Why? And what are you planning on doing with the money? If you are going to put it in the stock market, you don't need to sell it. You can rent it and turn it into an income. You can easily get $1,200 a month."

He promised he would not put it in the market. Well, he didn't like my ideas and said, "Just pray with me that it sells."

I said, "I can't do that," and that was that.

The next thing he did was gather the small boys in the room and ask them to pray with him. I walked in and could not believe my eyes. I told him not to use the boys, knowing God answered the prayers of the innocent. He told them that he would buy them an underground swimming pool if God heard and answered their prayers, and guess what? They had a buyer within the week. Did they get their pool? *No!*

Well, things turned for the worse when this happened. He did exactly what he said he wouldn't. He put every dime in the market and lost it all. We didn't even get a gallon of milk! I was crying. When you are married, it is not a one-way street, especially when an agreement is verbally made to each other to do one thing. God cannot bless you in that kinda thinking, and he wasn't blessed, and so we as a family weren't either. There is the human self getting in the way of doing right. Meanwhile, I was praying. Only God can change the heart.

CHAPTER 78

Turning Rotten

He slowly started to become very depressed. His phone hadn't really rung on a consistent basis in a long time. But wait . . . Wouldn't one expect bad things to happen when the motives are selfish? I will answer that. Yes, but he was the head of the household. Things were bad. We really had no money for food. I suggested that we see about food stamp assistance, for which we qualified. Oh, he thought this was great—no work, and they were feeding us! With our crew, it was a lot of food credit, I thought. I was sad that it had come to this.

I told him, "This is temporary assistance in a time of need. But it is not there for making a living. You need to go find work."

God's blessings died, but God wasn't the one who cut it off. He did by his actions. It literally became harder and harder where he could not find work. He lay around for days. The days turned into weeks, weeks turned into months, months turned into years, and years turned into more years. On and on, this went. I was still praying.

Chapter 79

His Online Feel-Good: "The Snake"

Choosing rather to suffer affliction with the people of God than to enjoy the pleasures of sin for a season. (Hebrews 11:25 KJV)

I got a phone call from a friend of mine.

"Are you still married?" he said.

"Yes. Why do you ask?

"Well, I saw a conversation with a lady on Facebook that is not appropriate. It made me think you were not married."

"Really? I need to go look."

Sure enough, there it was—all kinds of smut, inappropriate language for a married man to have with another woman, let alone make it a publication on Facebook, pure trash. He definitely was thinking between his legs and not with the heart.

I have a big piece of advice for you women who smile and flirt for all the wrong reasons with a married man. First, you'd better get a fear of God! He is the one who has the power to destroy you, and personally, God doesn't want you messing around with a married man. Girl, you are writing in your book that is found on the shelf in heaven. If you are single and desire a man, find one who is *not* married. Shame on you! Otherwise, you are a homewrecker, and it will come up in your book of remembrance. Do you love the Lord?

This lady swore she was a Christian. Ha! Meanwhile, she was calling her husband a snake. Who really is the snake here? On top of all this, when I confronted him, his response was denial, denial, denial. Problem? I got the evidence in black and white.

He changed the subject to say, "If you want to save this house, you are going to have to find work. I don't have the faith to believe anymore. If we lose the house, so be it. I will live in a trailer."

"This is ridiculous. Why would you lose a house that is almost paid for?" was my response. I went into shock and said, "I am not going down with your ship. I am getting off this sinking ship!"

He said, "If you want to save all this, you will have to do something. I am not! You need to save the Blue Cross insurance too!"

He was serious, and I needed help in my ever-present time of trouble. I knew the only way to save anything was with the Lord's help!

Chapter 80

Push

I had a vision of a man who was so huge, I could not take in his whole body. It was as if he were standing next to the earth, and we know how big it is. I could see his face. His hair was long, and he had a beard. He was good looking. He had on clothes that were of long ago, gray, blue in color. I wondered what he was doing standing there. He said nothing.

Then suddenly, he moved his hands in an upward position above his head. His massive arms were bent at the elbows, and his fingers pointed and came together in the center of his head. His arms took the shape of a massive heart because of his size. As he began to lift his hands away from his head, he held his fingers in a downward position. Going up, up, and up, as high as he could go, he moved his hands away, with his arms opened wide as if to represent wholeness. He headed downward to make a point at the base of his thighs, making a point with his fingers touching again. I realized he had just made a huge heart.

He turns the palms in an upward cup position toward me. He lifted his hands, and they met in the center of his body, exposing what I now clearly saw. I saw His nail-scarred hands. I realized it was Jesus. The words at this point were spoken, and He told me to "push, push, push!" The only time I was told to push was when I was having a baby. *Oh, God, am I giving birth to something new?*

He said, "Think of me and how much I love you. Push everything else out that is not from me. Push, rebuke, and leave it at the cross. Do this when you need to."

CHAPTER 81

Running Toward the Church

My whole being went into a tailspin, thinking about what my husband was doing, and it was not okay. I thought, *God, I am a Christian. This can't happen.*

"Oh, really? He is a man. Humans will hurt you," He softly said.

I had nowhere to turn except to God, and that is a great place to be. I dug in and refused to let go, even when I didn't feel the presence of the Lord, but I knew He was there.

> Be strong and of a good courage. Fear not nor be afraid
> of them, for the Lord thy God, he it is that doth go with thee.
> He will not fail thee nor forsake thee. (Deuteronomy 31:6 KJV)

I had to gather strength, and this verse was one of many I needed. I need to *push*—his mind (my husband), our lives, our children, our home. I was so overwhelmed that I completely freaked out. All I could think about was running to a church that very night! I got in my car and drove toward town, wondering, *What church, God? What church?* I knew there were several down the road. I literally drove down this one road, thinking one was tucked in the trees. There was nothing.

I drove out and saw a man covered in tattoos and said, "Is there a church down one of these roads?" with tears streaming down my face.

"Ma'am, I would not have a clue," he responded.

You need to get in this car and come with me to church, I was thinking. I thanked him and told him to make it a great day. I was sobbing. I drove off.

The church was the next block over. All New Beginnings was the name of this church. *Wow! Thank you, God. Really, God, you leave nothing unthought of, I thought. All New Beginnings! Thank you.* I sat quietly in my chair, hearing every word as if the message was straight from heaven. I fought back the tears. (I know that I am not the only one who has the Lord's Spirit talk personally in messages from the pulpit to us.) He is so amazing, and of course, I couldn't hold the sniffles.

When the service was over, I noticed a dear couple I had known in my early walk. In fact, they were my spiritual parents, the very ones who had taught me how to make Christmas bows. They played a big part in my born-again experience as well, cleaning my house of materials that were not of God, running everything by them, like "What does the Bible say about this and that?" (I was a baby and did not know. I was reading the scriptures, but that was going to take time.) I literally wondered if they would get tired of me asking so many questions. They were the most loving, God-fearing couple ever. What a precious family that God had provided!

Deliverance came, and they were one of four precious couples who felt called to help. Now that was an interesting time. I was a smoker, which I hated, and I was also a health nut, working out, watching food intake, and so on. I felt like a fake. No one knew I had this hidden problem.

One day I was reading my Bible, and the scriptures in Romans told me that there was something within me trying to destroy me. *Hmmm! Sin . . .*

> For we know that the law is spiritual, but I am carnal, sold under sin. For that which I do, I allow not, for what I would, that do I not, but what I hate, that do I. If then I do that which I would not, I consent unto the law that it is good. Now then it is no more I that do it but sin that dwelleth in me. For I know that in me (that is, in my flesh) dwelleth no good thing, for to will is present with me, but how to perform that which is good, I find not. For the good that I would, I do not, but the evil which I would not, that I do. Now if I do that I would not, it is no more I that do it, but sin that dwelleth in me. I find then a law that when I would do good, evil is present with me. For I delight in the law of God after the inward man. But I see another law in my members, warring against the law of my mind and bringing me into captivity to the law of sin which is in my members. O wretched man that I am! Who shall deliver me from the body of this death? I thank God through Jesus Christ our Lord. So then with the mind, I myself serve the law of God but with the flesh the law of sin. (Romans 7:14–25 KJV)

In other words, I read that to mean something in me was trying to destroy me. Wow! I was armed with the Word of God, and I planned on finding my freedom. I immediately contacted my spiritual parents, who went to a nondenominational church. It was the first time I had ever given a serious thought of what churches called themselves: Baptist, Catholic, Methodist, Church of Christ, Jewish synagogues, etc. Christ was not religious. He explained that religion is manmade. It becomes a tradition, a ritual, which is really an idol. The scriptures clearly say when you honor your father's tradition for the sake of tradition, you are making the Word of God void. It doesn't work. This is found in Matthew 15:6. *I am a believer in Jesus only.*

See to it that no one takes you captive by philosophy and empty deceit, according to human tradition, according to the elemental spirits of the world, and not according to Christ. (Colossians 2:8 ESV)

For the Pharisees and all the Jews do not eat unless they wash their hands, holding to the tradition of the elders, and when they come from the marketplace, they do not eat unless they wash. And there are many other traditions that they observe, such as the washing of cups and pots and copper vessels and dining couches. And the Pharisees and the scribes asked him, "Why do your disciples not walk according to the tradition of the elders but eat with defiled hands?" And he said to them, "Well, did Isaiah prophesy of you hypocrites, as it is written, 'This people honors me with their lips, but their heart is far from me. In vain do they worship me, teaching as doctrines the commandments of men.'" (Mark 7:3–9 ESV)

Preach the word. Be ready in season and out of season. Reprove, rebuke, and exhort, with complete patience and teaching. For the time is coming when people will not endure sound teaching, but having itching ears, they will accumulate for themselves teachers to suit their own passions and will turn away from listening to the truth and wander off into myths. (2 Timothy 4:2–4 ESV)

He answered them, "And why do you break the commandment of God for the sake of your tradition? For God commanded, 'Honor your father and your mother,' and 'Whoever reviles father or mother must surely die.' But you say, 'If anyone tells his father or his mother, "What you would have gained from me is given to God," he need not honor his father.' So for the sake of your tradition, you have made void the word of God. You hypocrites!" (Matthew 15:3–20 ESV)

Hear the word that the Lord speaks to you, O house of Israel. Thus says the Lord, "Learn not the way of the nations, nor be dismayed at the signs of the heavens because the nations are dismayed at them, for the customs of the peoples are vanity. A tree from the forest is cut down and worked with an axe by the hands of a craftsman. They decorate it with silver and gold. They fasten it with hammer and nails so that it cannot move. Their idols are like scarecrows in a cucumber field, and they cannot speak. They have to be carried, for they cannot walk. Do not be afraid of them, for they cannot do evil. Neither is it in them to do good." (Jeremiah 10:1–5 ESV)

Nor to devote themselves to myths and endless genealogies, which promote speculations rather than the stewardship from God that is by faith. (1 Timothy 1:4 ESV)

All Scripture is breathed out by God and profitable for teaching, for reproof, for correction, and for training in righteousness. (2 Timothy 3:16 ESV)

Knowing that you were ransomed from the futile ways inherited from your forefathers, not with perishable things such as silver or gold. (1 Peter 1:18 ESV)

You shall be careful therefore to do as the Lord your God has commanded you. You shall not turn aside to the right hand or to the left. You shall walk in all the way that the Lord your God has commanded you, that you may live, that it may go well with you, and that you may live long in the land that you shall possess. (Deuteronomy 5:32–33 ESV)

"This is the bread that comes down from heaven so that one may eat of it and not die. I am the living bread that came down from heaven. If anyone eats this bread, he will live forever. And the bread that I will give for the life of the world is my flesh." The Jews then disputed among themselves, saying, "How can this man give us his flesh to eat?" So Jesus said to them, "Truly, truly, I say to you, unless you eat the flesh of the Son of Man and drink his blood, you have no life in you. Whoever feeds on my flesh and drinks my blood has eternal life, and I will raise him up on the last day." (John 6:50–71 ESV)

As for the one who is weak in faith, welcome him but not to quarrel over opinions. (Romans 14:1 ESV)

I hope the scriptures above help explain traditional ways of religion. We are to be full of Christ and what He did for us. Looking at a Christian is like first looking at death. We die to ourselves. But wait! We are made new and alive in Christ. Yes, absolutely, and know we are not ashamed to love the conversation of telling others of His love. I am good if you think I am crazy 'cause I know I live, and I live in Him and have my being. Hallelujah! It's all good! ❤

Meanwhile, I called the church and told them my smoking problem, which I was hiding, and I wanted to quit. The Bible was personally talking to me on how and why I had this problem. I was so excited that I had the truth, and now I was going to be free from something I absolutely hated with a passion. But the stronghold had to be broken. I was told that they believed I was right under counseling. I went home and did the Daniel fast for three days, which was at sundown. I could only eat fruit and vegetables, and during the day, I could only have liquids, and I did it. It was the first time I had ever gone without food like that.

Prove thy servants, I beseech thee, ten days, and let them
give us pulse to eat and water to drink. (Daniel 1:12 KJV)

Oils proved to be very difficult, but I did it. The strangest thing happened though. It was like the demon of nicotine was upset. He had me smoking at least five cigarettes at a time. It was crazy. I remembered looking in the mirror with all five lit cigarettes hanging out of my mouth, and I was going to town, just a-puffing. Yuck! It was a sick feeling. That thing knew, and it was controlling me for the last time. I was so determined to free myself once and for all from the bondage those cigarettes had on me.

Three days had passed, and I met all who took part in my deliverance at the church. When I walked into the room in which we were praying in, I saw that a single chair sat in the center of the room. We wasted no time in dealing with the evil spirit. I sat, and they all gathered around and anointed me with oil. I absolutely came clean right there with the family of God. I confessed things I thought I could never confess. But I wanted to be free. I didn't want anything to stop the flow from heaven. I humbled my heart. I was redeeming what Satan was trying to steal from me: my life. Nine of us had to live in a bad situation. We just needed the Spirit of God to reveal the truth with the knowledge that He offered up to us. Wow!

And God created man in his own image. In the image
of God created he him. Male and female created he them.
(Genesis 1:27 ASV)

We were intended to be walking with God in the garden, but sin came, and Adam gave birth to a son who was now created in his father's sinful nature, bringing curses. But the great news is we are free in Jesus. Hello? Jesus was freeing me in His Word to rid the cigarettes. Oh, hallelujah! I was excited, to say the least, and I was not playing Satan's game. I was being given freedom. What a treasure!

I must emphasize that when I went into the building that day, three days prior to that, I absolutely had in my mind that I was going to be freed from this thing. I was not going to be a slave to the cigarette, which I had no desire to have. My flesh, I could not stop no matter how hard I tried, and I did try, and it did not work.

In other words, I wasn't taking no for an answer. I completely surrendered myself when I sat down in that chair. I thought nothing of myself except *You are not staying. You are coming out.* Once the prayer started, I remember shortly after, "the thing" actually started to talk out of my mouth. "We are not coming out. We like it in here."

The group of prayer warriors started to rebuke it. "You can't stay. She doesn't want you here. You have to go. We are commanding you out. In the name of Jesus, be gone!"

> And these signs will accompany those who believe. In my name, they will cast out demons. They will speak in new tongues.
>
> She was subject to you, for she did not know the real living God. Therefore, she walked in darkness.
>
> Wherein in time past, ye walked according to the course of this world, according to the prince of the power of the air, the spirit that now worketh in the children of disobedience. (Mark 16:17; Matthew 7:22; Luke 10:17; Acts 19:13; Matthew 12:27)
>
> She has freedom and liberty in Jesus Christ now! You have to go *now!* In the precious savior Jesus! (Ephesians 2:2 KJV)
>
> Now the Lord is the Spirit, and where the Spirit of the Lord is, there is liberty. (2 Corinthians 3:17)
>
> It was for freedom that Christ set us free. Therefore, keep standing firm, and do not be subject again to a yoke of slavery. (Galatians 5:1)

In the power invested in us through the Father, Jesus said, "Cast them out in my name, and they will flee in the precious power in the name of Jesus!"

I started to seriously choke. I didn't panic. I knew it was leaving, and I just sat there while the whole thing took place, totally surrendered to the idea of freedom. When it was over, I walked out free. I have not had one since, and that was thirty-two years ago. In fact, my lungs were cured as well. I had absolutely no sign of ever smoking. I was healed so well that when I got around a smoker, I literally choked and threw up. Wow!

CHAPTER 82

My Spiritual Parents

Back at the church, I was frantically looking for them that Wednesday night, and there they were in the church, in yet another one of my darkest moments in life. I walked over and could hardly contain myself. She asked how I was as we stood talking near the back of the building as others were leaving the building. I lost it. Tears flowed, and I told her what was happening and how I had to figure out how I was going to help my children and myself through this awful mess. My whole life was in the balance. The fear of the unknown was not fun. I had to find the good somewhere in all this.

> But as for you, ye thought evil against me, but God meant it unto good, to bring to pass, as it is this day, to save much people alive. (Genesis 50:20 KJV)

I could only think about my children, my family, my marriage, to try and save it and keep it holy. *Push!*

> Finally, brethren, whatsoever things are true, whatsoever things are honest . . . things are of good report. If there be any virtue, and if there be any praise, think on these things. (Philippians 4:8 KJV)

I was finding my smile with respect to my husband who was buried in the garbage he threw out.

CHAPTER 83

How Good Is God? Amazingly Perfect!

I had work.

The next thing I knew, a man walked over to me and said, "Hello. My name is Compassion and Mercy, with a mission for helping those who are misused and search for the God of Abraham, Isaac, and Jacob [not really, but that was certainly where my mind had taken me—wow!] I think I have a job for you."

I must have stood there in awe, just staring. Did I just hear that? The Boaz blessing! Hello? This story is in the Bible. It is of encouragement to see how God ordered Boaz to Ruth that day as she was out gleaning in the fields to feed her and Naomi. These footsteps were ordained by the Lord. Things don't just happen. We see where God led them and how He put them together. This is one of many favorite books, which also shares the greater insight that God will take care of *all* your needs. Just walk in His will—and what is His will? We will find it as we walk. Just thank Him for the beautiful day because it is. Your life could be the biggest mess. Just stop and go outdoors and just look, just breathe, feel the gentle breeze. In other words, forget yourself and find Him in your thanksgiving of life.

Meanwhile, about that time in my trance, I remembered his wife, Ruth, by the way, was one of five women mentioned in the genealogy of Jesus in the Gospel of Matthew, along with Tamar, who was widowed twice and yet didn't have a son. She was then promised another hand in marriage, but that promise was a lie. The second son slept with her but spilled his seed, which contained life, and this displeased the Lord, and he died. She tricked Judah and slept with him, and she produced a child. Judah was being disobedient by withholding what belonged to her and blamed her for his son's deaths. Judah was not going to let her have another son. He felt like she should be punished, but she brought out his staff, seal, and cord.

He was ashamed and said, "She is more worthy of me."

On Rahab, the "wife of Uriah" (Bathsheba), Ruth's heart would not allow her to separate from her now barren mother-in-law who had lost not only her husband but also her sons.

Ruth showed kindness toward her and told her, "I choose to stay. I choose to know your God whom you speak of, even though you question everything about your life and why this is happening to you."

Naomi returned to her land, and Ruth, well, she was not letting go and vowed to take care of her, and she did just that. Ruth is the model of compassion and willingness to have the same loving kindness that Christ showed us. This same kindness helped Naomi in her darkest moments and offered up a small glimmer of light—and, folks, that is all we need sometimes, to promote the well-being of others.

Ruth walked over, glowing with her first child in her womb. Compassion introduced her, and the words that flowed from his mouth quenched my dry and thirsty land. It was like a river of living water. I was so hurt and in so much pain. *Wow! Did he just say, "I think I have a job for you"?* I stood in awe, just staring. Did I just hear that? Immediately, my thoughts went to the starlight, to the Lord above, straight up to the heavens. *Only you can answer my prayer like this—and so soon.* I was so thrilled that I held back the tears—at least, I think I did. Heck, I may have been sobbing in gratitude and honor.

[Selfie time! (I don't think there were selfies at that time, and if there were, I didn't know about them.) To this day, I am not a big selfie fan. But I do know that my face had to have looked blown away and shocked. I know my heart was.]

He told me what the job would be.

I told him, "I have never done that before, but I'll tell you what. I will come to your plant and look at it, and if I think I can do it, I will, and if I think I can't, I won't."

He said, "That sounds fair enough."

As I was on my way to the plant that Thursday, I noticed the name of the road that took me to the plant. (The whole time, I was still in shock that I was going to look at a job.) The name was Union Road. I saw that and thought, *Wow! God, really?* I began to praise Jesus. *Union Road . . .* I drove down the long country road, with Southern cotton fields in full bloom, covering the earth in pure whiteness. I had serious reflection time to thank Jesus for his goodness, and here I was, on Union Road. *I am hearing the message. How beautiful!* I thought. Finally, I parked and went into the job site.

He showed me exactly what he wanted, and I told him, "I believe I can do it."

I did the work and was so thankful from the bottom of my heart. My family had money, money that was earned. It was more real money than I had seen in a long time. Boaz seemed happy with the work. I left and sent a thank-you in the mail.

I got a call out of the blue. It was Boaz about two weeks later.

He asked in a way so as to not offend me (Oh, if Boaz and his beautiful family knew how much this work will bless my family!), "Would you be interested in painting all nineteen machines? You did such a great job on the first one that the others look awful now!"

This call was certainly a godsend. Of course, I couldn't say no. My family needed the work. I was thrilled. I threw myself into work. I was able to try and keep myself busy and think about good and lovely things. My mind needed this. Remember, my husband had a girlfriend on Facebook, and I was completely broken. I just wanted to stay busy and not think about my life.

I was up and out the door at 5:45 a.m. I was the second one to show up at the plant. I worked every day until four. I was so thankful for the work but devastated about my life. I didn't want to think about it. It was very painful, yet staying busy and away from home helped me stay focused on what was important to me: family. I wasn't willing to give up on my marriage, yet he continued to talk with his girlfriend. I didn't allow him to sleep in the same room, and I prayed long and hard around the clock. Thank you, my precious family. You were the light that I needed in the darkest hour of uncertainty. ♥ I am forever indebted to you.

One day, on my way home from the plant, I was headed up the "highway to heaven," Highway 91. It had been a long day. I was wearing rags—literally dirty rags. Paint and black soot were everywhere on me.

I heard the voice of the Lord. I was having a conversation with the Lord when all of a sudden, He told me, "Pull the car over and get out on your knees and pray with your hands in the praying position."

Right here? Oh, Lord, please, no. What will the people think? I really had a very hard time thinking about this, and I really did not want to do this. But I knew it wasn't about me. So I did as He had asked. I pulled over, and I cried and prayed before the Lord. I really did not understand why He would have me put on this show. We are not to put on a show.

In fact, He said, "Go to your prayer closet and pray in secret."

So I did not understand this. But then again, we are not to lean on our own understanding.

CHAPTER 84

Behind the Number Thirteen

I was on the floor, working behind a machine numbered thirteen.

You might be saying, "Yeah, and why is the number thirteen important to insert here?"

Now I am not into numbers, but the Lord created the world and the fullness thereof.

> The earth is the Lord's and the fullness thereof, the world
> and they that dwell therein. (Psalms 24:1 KJV)

Numbers are a part of His creation. We can easily find a verse in the Bible with the references found with numbers. The Lord uses certain numbers over and over—seven, forty, thirty-three, and so on. Knowing this, I thought about the number thirteen. Jesus's ministry started at the age of twelve, when he stayed at the synagogue to teach the knowledgeable scholars, who were shocked at His wisdom.

- Number one is the self.
- Number two is love.
- Number three is communication.
- Number four is division/the freedom to choose.
- Number five is grace.
- Number six is family (people).
- Number seven is truth.
- Number eight is finances.
- Number nine is a high calling.
- Number ten is order, which goes back to oneself (you have to choose).

- Number eleven is from heaven to earth, which is two twos (double the love).
- Number twelve is one and two, which together are three, which is communication.

I was at the thirteenth machine. The number thirteen is often considered unlucky by those who are superstitious, but for angels, the number thirteen is very auspicious. As the combination of the numbers one and three, the number thirteen is a sign from your angels that you are connected to the ascended masters and their ability to help, one being the self (single), three being communication. Add them up, and you have four. Four is the divider. You have a choice to be free or be a slave.

God communicated to me something very profound, and He said it in four words. He gave me freedom through His son, Jesus. He divided me from the water birth to the supernatural birth, Christ, and communicated a liberty found in Him. His four profound words: "*I died for this.*"

Now here I was on the floor behind a machine numbered thirteen, and God was dealing with me. I was tucked away from the rest of the workers. I could hear the rain coming down on the tin roof. (If the story is true that the rain is God's tears, then we were both having a sincere moment of reflection of life.) Rainy days to me usually will bring comfort and relaxation. The blanket of dark clouds cover the sky, turning off the lights to say, "Relax, listen to the pitter-patter, and close your eyes." It almost always makes me sleepy. All I could do was dream and pretend my life was not falling apart at the seams. At least I had a job that kept my mind busy, and sleeping was not an option. I was finally needed. Boy, it felt good to be needed! I was so thankful.

I was on my knees behind that machine number thirteen when all of a sudden, I heard faint sounds that caught my attention and then more of a building of an eloquent symphony, softly playing instruments that we don't have here on Earth. I was allowed the privilege to hear this once before many years ago. I knew it was heaven's windows that had opened up to share this with me, and they did. *This is a very special time for the Lord, of course, to let me hear the softness in perfect harmony. This is music in heaven!* I said to myself.

The flute held a tune that seemed to never end. The melody was breathtaking, streaming like there was a peaceful brook flowing all around me. Such peace, a symphony of colors playing luminously and flowing in the atmosphere! Then came the flooding flow into the joining, as if one, the guitars and harps—like they too had voices. Oh, the melody was so calming, so beautiful, so harmonious, and it was being performed with perfection. I was engulfed like never before on the earth. *Beautiful, just beautiful!* As I bent over, with tears streaming down my face, I could hardly control myself in the presence of the Spirit of the Lord. He was moving right there behind the machine numbered thirteen. Such an elaborate instrumental composition in three or more movements, similar in form to a sonata but written for an orchestra and far greater, grander! I was allowed to hear this instrumental passage from the porthole of the heavens to the earth, raining down on me. Wow! I then heard a strong and powerful word that seemed to control me with all of my being. I tried to resist what He had asked me to do.

The Lord came all over me. He told me, "Get up and write these words. I give you for a song."

I said, "Lord, I can't do that. I am working at a plant for someone else. That would not be right."

He insisted, so I ran and found a pencil and paper and wrote these words:

Praise the Lord!
Let all the church bells ring!
Hear me sing, "Hallelujah to the King!"
"Before you were born, I knew all things!"
You are in His hands!
Sing to your King!
I, I, I love you!
Sing praise to your King!
He watches over you!
I, I, I love you!
The cord is hard to break . . .

Hmmm. I just wrote what I had heard. I did not understand what the cord was though. "The three-stranded golden cord is not broken by me." I will come back to this later in the story. I have to tell you this. Oh my gosh! He just gave me an answer to a feeling of who I am with Him on this earth. But first, let me finish the vision that followed.

After I wrote the words, I quickly went back to my spot. I had a vision behind the back of that machine. A feeling of pure sadness upset me so much. I was trying hard not to let anyone know I was weeping at that point. I could hardly catch my breath. *God, I know you love me, I know you care, and I know you are there.* These words were birthed that afternoon, and from that time on, I would say them whenever I was overcome with sadness.

There He was. He came and visited with me right there on the floor as I cried. He gave me a four-word sentence, and it was so profound. But first, let me please share with you the most beautiful story that was unfolding before my eyes. His body was given up so that we might live. I couldn't help but see the olive tone to His beautiful skin, which was kissed by His Father. He was magnificent to look upon as He gazed into my eyes. The God of heaven and of the earth conquered the grave. The Creator's Son was right before me. He had only one piece of clothing, a white covering that covered his man-ness. His hair flowed with shades of walnut that waved in the golden highlights that passed His broad, fit shoulders. Our eyes were locked. I was looking deep into *the* most beautiful blue eyes that illuminated the purest compassion of one's very soul that was running over, a love so deep that I can't really explain in earthly words the beauty unfolding in front of my eyes. Our eyes continued to look steadily and intently with great curiosity, great interest for both of us, pleasure and serious wonder.

I knew that the earth does not hold this, proceeding from God's only Son, His beloved. I, by the grace of God, was having a personal show of the greatest love ever. I am tapped into the divine laws, divine guidance, divine magnanimity, the heavenly, the divine kingdom. He had such an extremely awestruck moment with me. Wow! He knew I needed this message. I already understood the realness of Jesus. But . . . did I really? I was so moved. He had a present, and He was presenting to me a visual document of what He had done for sin. It was done. It was official. He was able to convey to my mind and heart to carry this with me, His compassionate love. He transported this truth from heaven to earth that day. He communicated and made known to me personally His love for us all. Wow!

Now I want to tell you. "I died for this." What is this? Whatever you are going through, big or small, He died for it, spiritual law to transfer truth. He owns it. Jesus, Jesus, this is you.

I found myself traveling back to the dry, thirsty earth that was stripping the flesh from our Lord, land through eternity, with no conception of time. In a flash, I was there, even to the depths of the deepest sea—so beautiful, so breathtaking, in every sense of the word. Oh, his eyes, bluer than any blue the world has ever known!

A wide-open space of nothingness, to the unseen eye, holds so much. *Dirt?* So much dirt surrounded him, His body, which was bent and twisted to see me. I stood there, taking it all in. His eyes continued to focus deep on my very being, as if nothing else mattered to Him but me. I saw His crown. It was brown vines that had been rolled many times to form a circle, twisted and wrapped over and over, creating a thickness of at least three inches with one-inch dark-brown spikes, at least an eighth of an inch in thickness, that poked out in every direction, drawing blood that drip profusely down on His precious face. His nose was slender and came to a slight point. His cheekbones were high, and his teeth were pearly white—just beautiful to behold.

Then I saw a man's forearm. It was as large as a man's thigh. His entire hand, fingers, and arm slid into the most beautiful glove of solid metals, bright colors of red and yellow, gold. It was a fine piece of artwork. It fit like a glove for the man wearing it. Then all of a sudden, I saw a whip that had many three-foot strips cut out of leather into many long one-inch-thick strips with one-inch-long silver and golden talons fastened every three inches down the thick strips. The Roman soldier had a skill in pulling back the whip over his head and threw with all his might, transferring all his energy into the whip into the back of Jesus, ripping off His flesh.

Then Jesus said, looking straight into my eyes, "*I died for this.*"

Wow! Wow! Wow! I knew this, but I didn't know this. It was a wow moment. Whatever you are going through, no matter how big or how small, He died for it. The Lord was bringing me comfort in my distressing time. I knew I had to trust. I knew I was nothing without Him. I knew that He formed me. I knew that He would never leave me. I knew that He was fighting my battles. I knew that Daniel waited only three weeks to hear back from the Lord. I thought, *I'll take three weeks, even though it has been years.* I figured that the unseen world must be awful on my behalf. I knew that God is with me even when I don't see it. I knew that He sees the pain. I knew to keep trusting, keep believing. *Win this race, for He is with you, Abigail, and He is made strong in your weakness.* I am choosing to praise you, Father, Son, and Holy Ghost!

CHAPTER 85

Oh My Goodness! I Am Cinderella

My lot in life—I went from riches to rags. Even in my riches, I cleaned my own home. I could've had a maid, but I loved taking care of my things. I found pleasure in it, really. I do recall my first cleaning job of another's property, and I wasn't there for that. I was hired to paint. I always had to clean the walls and baseboards before I could paint. These precious people even had regular cleaning services. I literally had to clean before I could paint.

I was asked by several people, "Do you clean?"

My response was "*No!*"

I went home and started thinking about it. *My other jobs are sporadic. Cleaning could be weekly, a regular paycheck.* I asked questions as to how often I would be needed to clean, and it was weekly. *Okay . . . I can fit in and still do my other work.* That was how that started, but my first stranger's toilet—really? *And the showers—yuck!* But my family needed the money.

I remember looking and scrubbing that first toilet. *Oh, God, my lot in life—riches to rags!* I was the toilet bowl scrubber that went round and round. To tell the truth, I was very sad yet happy to have work. So I scrubbed on. However, several families I worked for had nannies, and one of the little girls was testing her roots to see what it would be like to mistreat and not be kind to the nannies. I walked in, and they all shared their stories and were all crying.

"What's wrong?" I asked.

They began to tell me how the little girl was saying really awful things to them, making them feel just awful. I listened and reassured them that it would be okay. Well, later in the week, she decided to be unkind to me. *Oh, really?* I thought. After her harsh and ugly words, I looked at her and became very excited and was smiling and thanking her with joy.

"What? You are supposed to be sad," she said.

"Sad? Why?" I was happy, clapping my hands together with joy.

She was puzzled.

"Oh, this can mean only one thing. Thank you, thank you!" I took her hand and jumped for joy. "Thank you for letting me know I am Cinderella and my prince is coming for me."

"What?"

"Oh yes, you are the evil stepsister, and I am . . . I am *Cinderella!*" I started to dance in the room.

By this time, she was staring at me in total disbelief. "Wait! I am Cinderella! I am the princess, not you!"

I said, "That is impossible. Cinderella is kind, so kind that the animals talked to her and were her only friends."

Oh, the look on her face! It just flowed so perfectly from my lips that I knew God had orchestrated the whole conversation. She was near ugly again to anyone.

CHAPTER 86

The Five Lights Provided Suddenly

Meanwhile, I was staying busy with the remodeling of the house. I had bought some light fixtures for the house years back. But I realized I was short several others. I was working in a completely different part of the house. I worked one room at a time, and the basement wasn't even a concern. I had way too much to do upstairs. This took time because of resources.

One day I was driving along with my husband in the car, and I heard the still small voice, and it said, "Pull into the Lowe's and look for the lights you need."

I questioned this. I thought, *It was years ago when I had bought those light fixtures. They probably don't even sell that style anymore.* But I decided to go in the store. I knew that voice. I told my husband to pull over and let me run into the store real quick because I had just gotten word that I needed to go check on something. I went into the store, and to my surprise, there were exactly five clearance light fixtures. I needed five. There were the same exact ones I had bought years ago. There they were, sitting right in front of me for $10 apiece. I couldn't believe it. I was like, *Wow!* I bought them, and I knew that God had provided the same exact light fixtures that were upstairs and told me out of the blue to go into the store. Hello? He loves us in even the smallest of details. *This is awesome!*

Stay busy. Idle hands are the devil's workshop. Proverbs 16:27 tells us this. My mother must have known this. She always had us busy doing something. Idle lips are his mouthpiece—literally. "A worthless man devises mischief, and in his lips, there is a scorching fire."

Meanwhile, I was staying super busy with work. The Lord was providing an income that I didn't have to look for. It found me. Thank you, Jesus! My son needed knee surgery, and I took him to a bone doctor. For some reason, the doctor shared that he had built a house for his family, but they hadn't sold the other one yet. He told me where the house was that hadn't sold. So I knew right where it was. He mentioned that the recent housing crash hurt him, and he continued to say that he didn't have any money.

I kinda corrected him and said, "You at least are making the money to pay for what you do have. Look at it that way."

He said, "Yes, you're right," but he was trying to figure things out, I could tell.

I really thought the whole conversation was odd. Then it went into "Do you want to buy some great hunting land?"

"What? Do I look like a hunter?" *Does he possibly think I am in the market for a house? Hmmm. However, God knows what He is doing.* I just looked at the doctor and said, "Why don't we just ask the Lord for relief? Can I pray for you?"

He agreed. We prayed, and that was it, short and simple. *Father, give this family the relief you would have for them, and thank you for the money. He is making do. He doesn't lose what he has. Protect them so they can give you the glory.*

About a week later, I passed by his home that was for sale. Oh, I got really excited! A couple was poking around the property. I was so happy for the doctor, and I drove on. I had a job in the area that had me drive right by his home, and lo and behold—there was the same couple again. They looked serious about the home.

This time, I heard, "Stop and introduce yourself."

I said, "No, that is not going to happen," and I drove off.

The third trip into the neighborhood, there was a moving truck. *They are moving in! Yay!* I was so happy for the doctor that his home had occupants.

As I neared the house, I heard a voice say, "Go introduce yourself."

I said, "No."

As I drove completely past the house, a stern voice gave the order "Turn this car around now!"

Oh my! This voice means business! I did not want to find out what would happen if I didn't turn the car around. I knew that I had better listen and trust this voice that literally commanded me to turn around. I was so overwhelmed to follow and trust, even if it was way out of my comfort zone. This certainly was not something I would normally do.

I then said, "Well . . . if you are going to put it that way, I will."

I turned around, and my mind was going ninety to nothing. I was thinking over and over, *I cannot believe you are doing this.* The driveway was lined with boxwoods all the way up to the house. I got out of the car and walked up the wide stairway to the home.

The movers joked and asked, "Do you want a job?"

I said, "I don't think I can fit you in my schedule, but thanks," joking back to them. I just walked into the house, saying, "Hello? Hello?"

Finally, I heard a hello back. "We are in the kitchen."

The mother was there, helping her daughter unpacking with one other hired help. It looked like they were going to be very busy for a while, from the looks of it.

I said, "Hello, my name is Abigail, and I was just driving by and thought I would stop and say hello."

She introduced herself. "My name is Trinity."

"Oh, nice! That is my first daughter's name."

She said, "Oh. This is my mother and Hanna, my sister."

"Wow!" I immediately said. "My second daughter's name is Hanna."

About that time, her daughter came into the room. She was about Grace's age.

We talked about religion, and I mentioned, "Me? I am just a believer now. I don't believe that God divides people into certain groups of demonstrations. I am free from that."

"Oh," Trinity said.

I said, "Are you from the area?"

"No, we just moved here from Washington State."

"What? I was born and raised there. And I have lived here in Alabama for many years, and finally, today, after all these years, I meet someone from my home state. Wow! I could hardly believe it."

It was so perfect to me, and I knew God was right in the middle of it all. From everything she said, I knew we had some kind of connection. I thought, *God, you are so good*.

"Well, I think I should be going now. It was so great meeting you. Congratulations on your new job."

She walked me to the front door. Trinity asked, poking her head out the door, "Okay, which house is yours?" She looked around the yard. "Which house do you live in? It's nice to meet a neighbor so soon."

I said, "Oh, I don't live in the neighborhood."

"Oh, really?" she said. "I figured you were just coming in to say hello to your new neighbor."

"Oh, no. I was just driving by and saw you moving in. I was headed to a job here in the neighborhood."

She said, "Oh, what do you do?"

I said, "I am like a jack of all trades. I am not Jill. You know, Jack and Jill? I am a LuLu #1 of all trades. My daughter Hanna is Lulu #2. My motto is I will do anything as long as it is legal. I like my freedom."

She laughed.

I dug around in my purse and pulled out a business card. "I thought that the house could use some fresh paint on the walls."

She asked, "Are you married?"

I said, "Yes, but I feel like I have been thrown to the world. I am going through a very dark time in my life. And I would not wish this on an enemy."

"Oh. Here is my email address. Please send me a résumé. I'll see what I can come up with."

She reached for me and gave me the biggest, most precious hug ever. We smiled, and that was it. As soon as I got into my car, I stared in disbelief. I was in a trancelike state, and my hands gripped the steering wheel and rolled out, following the long curved driveway. I started to thank the Lord. I literally cried. I just couldn't believe how it fit like a perfect glove. She was very warm, and at that time in my life, I was on shaky ground. I had so much responsibility, and my husband was off on a wild internet ride. I didn't want my marriage to end, so I just kept busy and prayed.

Weeks went by after sending her my résumé—nothing. I thought, *If it is meant to be, it will be.* Then one day, out of the blue, the phone rang. It was Trinity. She asked if I would be interested in working three days a week—Monday, Wednesday, and Friday. It worked out perfectly. The hours she needed did not interfere with my other clients. *How perfect! God is so amazing!*

Trinity was later confused that her sister had said, "Do not hire that lady. That is just weird, how just walks up to someone's house and starts a conversation with you and does not even live in the neighborhood."

Trinity said, "Yeah . . . but there is something about her." (Awww, sweet!)

God took me to that house that day. I had even told Him that I was not going to do that. Can you imagine?

CHAPTER 87

The Power of Prayer

One day all the boys were headed to a homeschool baseball game, and three were on the same team. My work schedule would not allow me to go. They all piled in a gray Oldsmobile that their grandma had given their daddy. The time was around two thirty in the afternoon. I was busy working for Trinity that particular day. About this time, I was asked by Trinity to pick up her children from school that day, which I rarely did. I wasn't finished with my day at her home yet. But it wasn't a big deal. I certainly could run and pick them up.

As I was driving, my daughter Grace was in the car, and I heard suddenly an urgent order: "As soon as you get into the parking lot, go straight to the church and pray."

I realized that someone I love was going to be in trouble. I didn't know who, but there was an extreme urgency. Angels needed to be dispatched, but I dismissed the actual need to go into the church. *I don't need to go into the church, Father. I can pray in the car. I can pray right here right now. Besides, I am working for someone. They are not paying me to pray. And I don't want to keep the children waiting. I have to be in line and wait.*

Immediately, I heard, "Go into the church and pray."

There was such an urgency. I looked at the clock and thought, *Well, I have just a few minutes to do this and get back in line.* It felt like a beeline.

Grace asked, "What are we doing, Mom?"

I said, "Just get out of the car, please. We have to go in here quickly."

I parked and grabbed Grace's hand and ran into the church. I did the respectable thing and told Grace to dip her finger on the sponge and place the water as I did, making the shape of a cross, saying, "The Father, Son, and Holy Ghost." She did it as perfectly and quickly as I did.

All I said was "Jesus, there must be a family member or friend in trouble.

Now I don't have time to figure it out. But you know what it is and where we need angels to go now to assist whoever it is. Send them, however many it will take to protect them, whoever it is. Thank you for loving us so dearly. Amen. In the precious name of our Lord and Savior, Jesus Christ."

We ran back to the car and got in line, and I was not late. The children came out and got in the car, and we drove off. We were all talking about their day, and the phone rang.

"Hello." The voice on the other end of the line was breathing in disbelief as he explained the serious situation they were in. "Oh my gosh! I don't know how we managed to escape or managed to survive a head-on collision. A woman and I were going around eighty miles an hour when we should've crashed. But my car just did some kind of crazy maneuver, and we made it out alive!" my husband exclaimed.

Listening intently, I asked this one question, which I already knew the answer to: "Did the children have on seat belts?"

He said, "No."

I immediately praised the Lord for saving my children. Can you imagine getting a call to tell you that your family was killed in a wreck? *This is seriously serious stuff!*

Then I said, "I know exactly why you and the children are all safe. Just moments ago, God had me run into a church and ask for protection for someone I love. I knew it had to be bad, whatever it was. There was such an immediate urgency to pray that came all over me. I was in the church, praying for their protection."

See, Satan had a plan, but God rejected it! He gave me knowledge to pray. Now had I not prayed, God forbid, my worst nightmare would have been getting a call that your sons were all dead. Oh, I praise Him! See how He loves us so? Remember when Wolfgang was young and I told God no? My son suffered. He was training me to hear and act on His still small voice.

Thank you, Father, for your truth and protection, even into the fullness of the future, knowing and acting on that knowing. We don't have to know all the details unless He wants us to.

CHAPTER 88

I Dreamed of My Father's Death

Now let's go back to the beginning of the story, when I had mentioned that God is about new beginnings. We are in the stars and in the sand through the generational blessing, brought through the blood of the Lamb. Abraham knew this and the saints before. A Gentile grafted in.

I dreamed of my father's death. He passed away, and I woke with the thought that I couldn't let him die without sharing what Jesus had done for us. This was a very uncomfortable feeling, calling my father and talking with him about the most important decision of one's life, but I knew I had to do it. I took a big breath and dialed his number.

"Dad, hi. This is Abigail. How are you? Oh, I miss calling you!"

He was having hearing problems, and when I called, I literally had to yell at him, which upset me. I fought the tears. I felt an urgency that I wasn't sure when he might pass.

"Dad . . ." I took a deep breath. "I have a question." I was shaking and trying not to cry, but that wasn't going to happen. The tears were flowing.

"Yes?" he said.

"Do you know what 'born again' means?"

He laughed. "Yes. Yes, I do. Are you crying?"

"Oh, no!" I was lying.

"You must think I am going to die."

"Oh, no, Dad. We could all die at any moment. God forbid!" I was still lying.

"Why do you ask?

"Well, it is just important to know."

He began to tell a story. "I asked Jesus in my heart when I was fifteen after a corn-husking party. Back in those days, there wasn't a whole lot to do, and farmers needed help with shucking the corn, and the townspeople all met at the church. That was the extent of fun for us. And really, it was fun. We would make a game out of it."

I was so relieved to hear this, but I was also perplexed. "Wow! That is a great, Dad. But why did you not share your born-again story with any of your children? That was probably the most important conversation you would have with your children."

He proceeded to say, "I married your mother. The church had me sign a document stating I would never share my faith. And the only reason we are having this conversation is because you are asking me now. You asked. I am telling you."

I quickly realized I didn't want to condemn him for not sharing, and I reverted and said, "Oh, Dad, this means you are a man of your word." I tried to explain that I was thrilled for him and so relieved.

We stopped the conversation on the subject. After hanging up with him, I realized that my dad had bottled up his faith for years and never shared his real faith. I praised Jesus for the dream, and I realized the purpose of the dream was so my father could state from his mouth the confession that Jesus was alive and in his heart, hidden all these years. How beautiful!

I understand that after the phone call, he read his Bible for a year before his death. God is so perfect. He used a dream to have him share the most precious news ever. *Born again at fifteen!* He passed, and shortly after, I had a vision that was so real. He was absolutely filled with his youthfulness. He was restored. He was sitting in the grandstands, watching and cheering. He was so excited. Then suddenly, he leapt from the stand with such an overwhelming joy, clapping his hands as if to say, "Keep up the good work of sharing the greatest news ever. I was rebirthed, and now I am here from the grandstands of heaven, cheering you on."

Thank you, God, for the assuring assurance I have with you. God has a way to get to us. We must listen. I don't even want to know what would have happened without the obedience to pray. Prayer does change things, even if we don't understand, but obviously, it is real.

CHAPTER 89

This Day, November 21, 2019 — The Father, the Son, the Holy Ghost, and Me

I am choosing to love from heaven to earth to all of humanity. The Father's Son makes known His will and reveals the truth to us all, which, in return, brings joy unspeakable. We can express the richness of His love, His Son, *Jesus*. My dedication is to the one who gave it all, Jesus. To tell you what I believe, this something beautiful was spoken many moons ago.

I may not be the prettiest girl on this stage, but I feel like the prettiest with all the support and comfort in all the ones who really helped me, the ones who made me dig deeper to find strength and courage when I had dropped to 120 pounds, being five feet and nine inches tall. I was nothing but skin and bones. But, Southern people, you embraced me. You prayed for me and were with me on many occasions. You saved my life from sin when I didn't know the truth. I thought I was going to heaven, being baptized as a baby. You told me that I needed a personal relationship with Jesus and that my sins could be thrown into the sea, never to be reminded of again. You kept me busy from the life that was from hell. It amazes me how God brought all of you into my life and quietly supported me, wondering deep down, *Is she going to make it?* Many of you thought the stress of it all would kill me, you shared years later. But through all this, I know that my life isn't the only life that is suffering in pain for whatever reason.

I want to share my story and give back to all of you, those who don't know what I have found through you all and your commitment of the love you found in Christ. You freely gave me sound advice from the Holy Bible. You helped me find what I once had and to go deeper in my faith and helped me become stronger and not lose hope. You helped me make this book happen. I want to share my story to help another, just as you have helped me, and let others know that they are not alone. You are the ones who helped me know Christ when I moved to the South. Meeting these beautiful people in the South, I can truly say they are definitely servants to the Most High God. I love you all so!

Drum roll—and who are you? I want to thank all the negative influences too—my childhood acquaintances, the one who made me look for Jesus in the first place, the one who made me stronger, the one who made fun of my name growing up, the one who told me I was stupid, the one who threw rocks at me for no reason, the one who made fun of my nasal voice, the one who made me feel unloved, the one who taught me that people are human and will hurt others for their sick pleasure, the one who stole my virginity when I was too young to understand (Pervert! You know who you are, and just to let you know, I didn't tell anyone because I knew my precious father would have found you out and blown your head off, and I protected my father from going to jail for murdering you. You pervert!), the one who was mad when I talked, the one who broke the bonds of marriage. I thank you. You made me search for something bigger than life.

CHAPTER 90

The Dream That Turns into a Vision — The Earth Breathes

It was early morning, and my dream was in full force. At that time in my life, I had been praying for a son of mine who had gone down a road that was not God. My heart was heavy and sick. *Oh, God . . . not another one.* I realized that we cannot make anyone change. Only the power of prayer can do that. I pressed on in prayer, trusting and rebuking anyone and everything that was coming against him. *Push. This is not an easy place to be.* Every waking moment, I was lifting up him and others in my life and trusting the Lord to hear my prayers.

Then suddenly, I saw something floating in the atmosphere. I was going with the flow, but I was very uncomfortable. It was dark swirls of what appeared to be smoke but had no smell. In the distance, I saw a gigantic pear shape with deep black craters running down the whole entire thing like volcanic death. There was not one thing of life in or near it. I knew instantly it was evil. As I got closer, I saw that the thing was expanding, opening, and closing. At the top, the hole, it was breathing. I then saw two white ghost hands floating in the atmosphere. I knew those hands had no life and that they were dead. The hands were gravitated toward the opening while all along, that thing was breathing, opening and closing. It was so creepy.

Then I heard a voice that kept saying, "The light has gone out. The light has gone out."

I began to weep uncontrollably, begging God to wake me up. *I don't like this dream, God. Please wake me up. Please, God, don't let these hands be Preston's. Please, God. He is young and has his whole life ahead of him. He has gone down the road wrong, but that is only because of human rejection. He once called you his. He gave his life to you. Please, God.*

Please don't let this be Preston. Then suddenly, I was wide awake. I was sobbing and frightened, for whoever this was, it was not good.

But the voice said, "It is too late . . . The light has gone out. The light has gone out."

Meanwhile, the hands drifted toward the opening, being sucked in, these ghost hands with no color, stark white. I thought, *God, really, why are you doing this to me? It was a terrible dream, and now I'm wide awake, and it's a vision? I am not liking this at all.* I thought by waking, the dream would go away. But to my surprise, it continued on while I was awake. I was now sitting up in disbelief in my bed, sobbing and crying, trying to catch my breath.

As soon as the hands were sucked in, there was a line around the rim of the hole of this breathing thing. It was a tiny light, so tiny, so thin that it was odd, but as it closed, the light formed in the shape of Jesus's name clearly.

As it was closing, I could see the name of Jesus, and as I saw the name of Jesus, I heard the voice repeating, "The light has gone out. The light has gone out."

Then the opening closed, and I knew the hands were gone forever. Jesus's name faded—gone. *Poof!* No light. Then I suddenly saw a concrete slab was placed over the hole. Out of nowhere, sinister hands appeared and started to stroke and pat the concrete. As it was stroking the concrete, it was affirming, "I have you now. You are mine!" I knew it was not good.

I wept and wept and wept for whoever's hands those were, and I just knew they belonged to my son. I continued to beg the Lord for mercy, and then I demanded to know who those hands belong to. *You have to tell me whose hands, God. Please. Please tell me they are not my son's. You gave me this vision, this dream, and now I have to know.*

I immediately heard, "The one without the fingertip."

I knew instantly whom these hands belonged to. They were not my son's hands. *Thank you, Jesus.* If anyone knows the Lord and turns from Him and has tasted His goodness and takes others with them as they turn, that is a dangerous place to be. The scriptures actually say this will require your very life. Since this dream/vision, the Lord has done mighty, mighty work in my son's life. In fact, it needs to be book three, titled *Please, God! Don't Let That Be My Son!* I would like to tell his story. God is an amazing, Father. Preston and the good Lord are turning things around for the good of those who love Him.

The enemy wanted him badly, but the enemy couldn't have him. He threw every obstacle in his way that he could find, staring with certain bad people. But God had him and protected him and is working miracles in his life right now. God gets all the credit because only God can turn this around, and prayer was the way to lift him up. Remember this if your life is so bad that you think there is no hope. Guess what? That is Satan saying that to you because he does not want you to find the greatest Savior and His plan for you. This is why we struggle. Know the truth, and the truth will set you free. That is a promise.

CHAPTER 91

Went on a Whim — Raising up Mighty Warriors (I Am Raising Up David's)

One day, after a long week of work, my dear friends had mentioned a meeting that was taking place in a home nearby. A prophet of the Lord was coming into town, and they had met at this home. Anyone in the town was invited to come, and I had heard of it that day for the first time. It was a Christian meeting, a worship service, and the taking of the Lord's supper. I thought, *I really want to go to this.* I finished out my day and met them back at their home. It worked out perfectly. Really, God is about being perfect because I've seen Him many times work things out perfectly. I left my car there, and we drove on, the three of us.

When we got there, we were told of a testimony of the owner of the home. When he was young, he was stricken with cancer. He was a very young man, with a new wife and possibly a baby on the way. He wasn't feeling well, so he went to the doctor, and the doctor discovered that his body was covered in cancer and that there wasn't anything they could do for him.

He looked at him in dismay and said, "There's nothing you can do for me?"

"No, I'm sorry. Do you have a Bible? If you have one, you need to go home and read it because God is the only one at this point who can heal you. You should be gone within thirty days."

It was bad. He went home, and he read his Bible, and he was believing in God for healing. *I'm sure. I'm sure of it.* That was the only place he could turn. Then one night he felt this current running through his body, but he didn't think anything of it. He thought it was just the cancer eating away at him. Then the second night came. The same thing happened. He could feel this current running through his body again and didn't think anything of it. He just thought it was cancer. Well, the third night came, and he felt the electricity again, but this time, he knew that the Lord was healing him. He confirmed it through the doctor. He was cancer free.

He opened his house up for the ministry of the Lord. He shared his testimony, and the Lord gave him a new song and an awesome family to go with the song. What a wonderful life! The Lord healed him completely. Not only did he bring healing physically, mentally, spiritually, and financially, but also, he brought in people with an inheritance for the kingdom through his testimony and through opening his home to hear the Word of the Lord. God used him to bring glory in. God is alive, and He is well. He wants to heal you right now. I can honestly say that because that's just who He is. Do you have a Bible? If not, please get one and read it. He gives us more than we could ever think or ask.

Meanwhile, I was there at the home. It was a beautiful home, by the way. The Lord had richly blessed him and his family, and we were listening to the prophet and were into the meeting.

She stopped, and she was calling for prayer, and she said, "There's a woman in this room, and her name is Abigail."

Abigail? Me? I sat there, and I thought, *She's not calling me. There's another Abigail here.* So I sat, and I waited and waited, and no one came forward.

She said again, "Is there an Abigail in this room? You need to come up here."

At that point, I stood up, and I said, "It's me, but I thought maybe somebody else was in the room who needed this message, so I didn't come forward."

"No, it's you. Come up here." So I went up to the front of the room, and she told Ashley, "You are going to pray for her."

I was instantly connected to this woman as she walked into the room earlier that evening. It was like this magnet, which was strange, and she said, "You're gonna pray for Abigail." She was standing there, and she was looking at me, and in her mind was *Okay, how am I going to pray for this woman?*

"God, you know where she has parked her life. What do you want to pray for in her life?" she began to pray.

She put her hands on me, and I was receiving the words, and all of a sudden, as I was closing my eyes, I heard a mighty sound of charging horses. I mean, it was loud. The earth was shaking. There were so many horses. I was just taking it in, so I could see them approaching. They were dressed in the most magnificent robes in jewels. I mean, it was over the top, and the colors were just gorgeous. The men on the horses were dressed in purple, gold, and red, just beautiful colors. Royal colors were the best of the best, and there was a banner in the center that the rider held tightly. As the banner blew in the breeze, it had this word: *Restorations.*

They dismounted, and I saw a sea of men's heads. They were packed together. That was all you could see of them. I just saw the heads of the men, nothing but the heads, and I thought, *Wow!* Then they moved apart. They fell to their knees, crying out to the Lord in repentance, true repentance.

I said, "What is this?"

The Lord said, "I am raising up mighty warriors. I am raising David's. Total restoration of the men. They will love me, and in turn, the world will respect the men. Order is coming back. Men will honor the family and the people because they fell and repented and desire to really know me. They put me first in everything. Total restoration! I am coming back for a church that is in one accord, and that is order and the highest calling of love."

That was it. She stopped praying, and I told the woman praying for me what had just taken place in the vision. She looked at me and told me about the very same vision she had had three months before, when she was in prayer with the Lord.

Get ready, men, to take back what belongs to you with the love of the Lord Jesus by your side. He is the master designer of order. Rejoice the things to come that the Lord has for you. *Push.*

CHAPTER 92

The Travel Mobile — I Could Not Have Done This Without You

I had a dream that became a vision. Oh, I love those messages! I was youthful looking and almost as beautiful as y'all. I was given a car. Its name was the Travel Mobile. Oh my gosh! It was a beautiful soft pink and a very special car. It was like no other. It was one of a kind, trimmed in a shiny chrome and flat black. I was standing there, admiring it with my friends. We were in awe, just standing, there staring and talking about this beautiful car.

Then suddenly, the windows opened up like a crystal-clear wall that had no end. I realized that we were looking into God's creation as far as forever went.

Then simultaneously, the words flowed from our mouths as we looked at one another: "I could vacation in that."

Guess what? We are all traveling down those roads. But what do you see on your road in your car? How do you respond to others on your road? You are the car. You are in the Travel Mobile. Believe in the supernatural because it is the unseen that God wants to manifest to us. The roads we travel are covered in His blood. We are covered. I actually had a vision on this, but I am going to stay focused, just as my chosen friend and I remind each other.

"Stay focused," my friend said. ♥

Our lives are free to live how we want to. All His gifts are free. Man is the one in charge of his life. Jesus fully respects you. You choose. The beauty of His creation is willed to us to travel on. What we do with it is our story. Our roads belong to Him. He owns it all, and He is rich, rich, rich in every aspect, in conversations. He is in the power behind the waterfalls. We are rich in the very meaning of life. Yes, yes, and yes—rich in the true sense of having Christ, who is the fullness of our riches. Yes, absolutely!

In life, we have to have money to travel. But God created everything. Shouldn't we trust Him to provide? He wants us to be the hands and feet to carry the Word of God to those who do not know the Word of God and yet even to those who do know the Word of God to grow even more in one another. It is called fellowship. In trying to be everything that we can be, we sometimes find ourselves in a big mess. Women try to be beautiful, and they don't have to try hard because they are beautiful. Beauty is of the heart.

In the dream that I had, I was really just going here and there and trying to do all the stuff and trying to be altogether and trying to have the right hairdo, to have the right dress, to have everything right. Sound familiar? This and that and tit for tat. The blue jean dress in my dream had been worn for days. My suitcase was lost.

In fact, when the day had finally arrived, I looked at myself and said, "Great!" I was a big mess on the outside, but on the inside, all I wanted to do was share the love of God.

Suddenly, everyone was encouraging me to do this. We scurried to get to the destination. I was worn out. The day of acceptance was finally here. My hair was a wreck. My dress literally had too many muddy handprints that you can see plainly, right there, for the whole world to see. My acceptance dress was lost in my suitcase. Well, a dear friend was doing everything in her power to get it. I remember stopping myself and literally picturing her in my mind and envisioning all she was going through to help me win. In fact, she was also in the race to win, yet she was encouraging me to win. I was defeated, looking at her. She was so beautiful and looking at me. Oh, what a mess! But she came to me, and she found it—my dress. She drove up to me in my pink Travel Mobile. There she was. She showed up in my car. That was an awesome sight to see (her, not the car). She spun the car around like she knew what she was doing right there in front of me.

"Wow! I am impressed. You sure can drive that car well." I asked her, "So what are you doing?"

"I found your dress!" She laid it down in front of me.

I put it on and in a hurry as she drove down the road to get me to my acceptance speech. Men were everywhere, all around, not really moved by what we were trying to do, and not one man cared to help. They were in the world pumping their physical muscles and making themselves strong. I don't understand that part of the dream because men do care.

There was a preacher who was going to give a speech, and his assistant was there. I remember he gave a long speech and ended it with "Where is the King?" He walked around, saying, "The King is going to be very upset because we used His plates. Someone used the wrong plates."

I looked at him in his frantic state, and I realized that those were the plates we were to have and to use. Those plates belonged to the King. He wanted us to use them. He wanted us to show the world that He had everything and that He was here all along.

The assistant walked away, mumbling and worrying himself sick that he couldn't relax over anything. He was so self-condemning, wondering what the King was going to say or do to him. Sad. His life was in a container that filled up, but he closed it off because he had a lid. The potter could not put anything more in because he limited himself with doubt and murmurings. Therefore, his road was not overflowing, like Christ said it could.

Meanwhile, I looked down at my red velvet dress, long and flowing. It looked like the dresses that were worn in the ancient days. No one, not one, was wearing anything remotely close. Their dresses were modern-day dresses of the time. I looked, and I thought, *You've got to be kidding me.* It was even wrinkled from sitting. I said to myself, *I've got to get to my next important meeting of my life.* Then suddenly, I thought it wasn't the dress, the fake lashes, the perfect hair, the manicured nails (even though all that were nice). It was and is about the race and how and what we do to get there. But then all of a sudden, the King appeared and was looking around. I thought, *What? Why am I here? Why do I think that I can win?*

Then suddenly, I remembered thinking, *I didn't get here by myself. It was from the help of those who cared to share their time and their own personal love stories of how a King took them from the deepest, darkest moments of nothingness and showered them in His love. We have wonderful people who comfort us with the Word of truth, to free us from ourselves! He has done work in them and will continue to do work in us.*

He was sharing with me how the Father loves me, us, you, and everything in between. I listened in awe. *Really? He can love me like this?* He promised He would never leave me nor forsake me. *Wow!* Their concern for me and my life mattered, to tell me I was a daughter of the King and I was loved by the King. Wow! He would take all this unwanted baggage and cast it into the sea if I will only let go. These beautiful people hired me when I had no money.

They helped me stay busy and think on the Father's love through the resources that were being provided, and in my darkest hour, they were the light of hope. They were the salt of the earth, giving me a sweet fragrance of the glorious King. They put light on the jewels that God saw in me and I now see in you.

The still small voice spoke to the frantic mode I was in. "Be still and know you are loved."

God brought people to help me have a will to win the love that was everlasting, which would never fail no matter how we looked to others. It works, the power of prayer

> Is any among you afflicted? Let him pray. Is any merry? Let him sing psalms. There is a time and a season for all things under the sun!

My own husband abandoned me. Strangers in the Lord fed me, clothed me, even gave me jewelry.

Chapter 93

The Pearls

One day I was at a precious lady's home, cleaning. I had on my rags—and I mean *rags*. She had all this jewelry out on a table. I thought, *Wow! How beautiful.* There was a piece that I commented on. Not thinking much about it, I went on about my work. Moments later, she called me over and had the piece in her hands.

She wrapped it around my neck and said, "There! It is absolutely beautiful on you."

"What?" I danced in my rags.

"Ta-da! It is yours."

I knew she was trying to earn money by selling some of her prized possessions. I walked over to my wallet to see what I had. It wasn't much, a $20 bill. I handed it to her and said, "It isn't much."

She expected it and said, "Oh, honey! Those are real pearls. Enjoy it. I know you will."

I was later sitting down at a concert and was wearing them. I looked down and saw that there were eight pearls and one green stone in the center. I realized that I had eight pearls, one for each child. I had had a miscarriage, and the green stone represented the lost child whom I could have the hope of seeing again one day. Wow!

When I was turning thirteen, for my birthday, my mother pierced my ears. She had given me two pearl earrings, one for each ear. They were very special indeed. One night I slept over at a family member's house. I left them on the coffee table because I had slept on the couch. I woke up, and they were gone. I was sick, forever sick. I later found out that my sister's husband had a girlfriend and that he had given them to her as a gift. I never saw them again.

But years later, the Lord brought this wonderful lady and blessed me with the most precious gift ever—the pearls. Wow! God gave me more than I could think or ask. Thank you, sweet friend who helped me in one of the toughest times in my life for my beautiful pearl necklace.

I am changing the subject for just a second. Did you know that there are twelve gates to heaven and each one is made of a single pearl? Can you imagine the intricate work in the carvings? Can you imagine the massive size of the pearl? Wow! The twelve gates represent the twelve tribes of Judah.

Is any among you afflicted? Let him pray. Is any merry? Let him sing psalms. There is a time and a season for all things under the sun!

And the prayer of faith shall save the sick, and the Lord shall raise him up, and if he have committed sins, they shall be forgiven him. Confess your faults one to another and pray one for another that ye may be healed. The effectual fervent prayer of a righteous man availeth much. Elias was a man subject to like passions as we are, and he prayed earnestly that it might not rain, and it rained not on the earth by the space of three years and six months. And he prayed again, and the heaven gave rain, and the earth brought forth her fruit. (James 5:13, 15–18 KJV)

CHAPTER 94

The Kite Made of Three Strands

Through all that people face—death, cancer, job loss, divorce, unfaithfulness, all the uncertainties of life—I personally felt like a tiny speck in a giant world, and I imagined I had a string that connected me to heaven and I was hanging on for dear life. I was not letting go no matter what. That was it. That was all I had, my tiny string that faded in the distance, high above the realm of heaven, and I was a speck on the earth.

One day the Lord explained, "If you look closer, it is not a string. It is three golden cords that are not easily broken. They are wrapped together—the Father, the Son, and the Holy Ghost. The only way the cord appearing as one can be broken is you breaking them. The only sin that can't be forgiven is blaspheming the Holy Spirit."

What is blasphemy? Impious utterance or action concerning God or sacred things, Judaism, an act of cursing or reviling God, the pronunciation of the Tetragrammaton (YHVH) in the original, now forbidden manner instead of using a substitute pronunciation such as *Adonai*, theology, the crime of assuming to oneself the rights or qualities of God, irreverent behavior toward anything held sacred, priceless, etc. He uttered blasphemies against life itself.

CHAPTER 95

It All Started with a Search of God Many Years Ago

"God, how am I going to do all this? My whole world that I know is uprooted, my comfort, my safe haven. We all have struggles, right? Of course, we do. That is life—but wait. I am a Christian. This cannot be happening to me and my family."

Oh, really? Guess what? Things happen. But this is where the test really starts. What are we really made of? People will hurt us. They are *human*—human, I tell you. This is why we need a Savior, so we can lay down our lives in Him, so we can live. How beautiful are the feet of those who share the gospel of Jesus Christ, Him beaten, crucified, buried, and raised from the dead for us! ♥

My feet are not so pretty, callous everywhere. I once had a dancer tell me she wished she had my feet.

"What? Why?"

"You have dancer's feet!"

Gee, thanks! That is good to know. This life is a dance!

> For whosoever shall call upon the name of the Lord shall be saved. But how can one call on Him if you don't first hear the good news? How can you believe if you don't hear what to believe in? Jesus sends believers into our path for a reason. Why? So you can hear! Remember, it is written, "How beautiful are the feet of them that teach the Word of God that is peace and bring joy to the hearts that need to hear the hope that is found in Him, which offers help in all things, through the Son who gave it all!"

I found this to be true in my life, and I would like to share the same good news with you. ♥ I know you will share the awesome news to others too. Where your natural father or natural mother fails you, God, who gave us the greatest gift, does not. Find grace and know that He certainly loves (♥) you. It is finished! Love to y'all. Roll Tide!

Made in the USA
Las Vegas, NV
14 July 2022

51576876R00146